THE KILLING GROUND
Wilderness to Cold Harbor

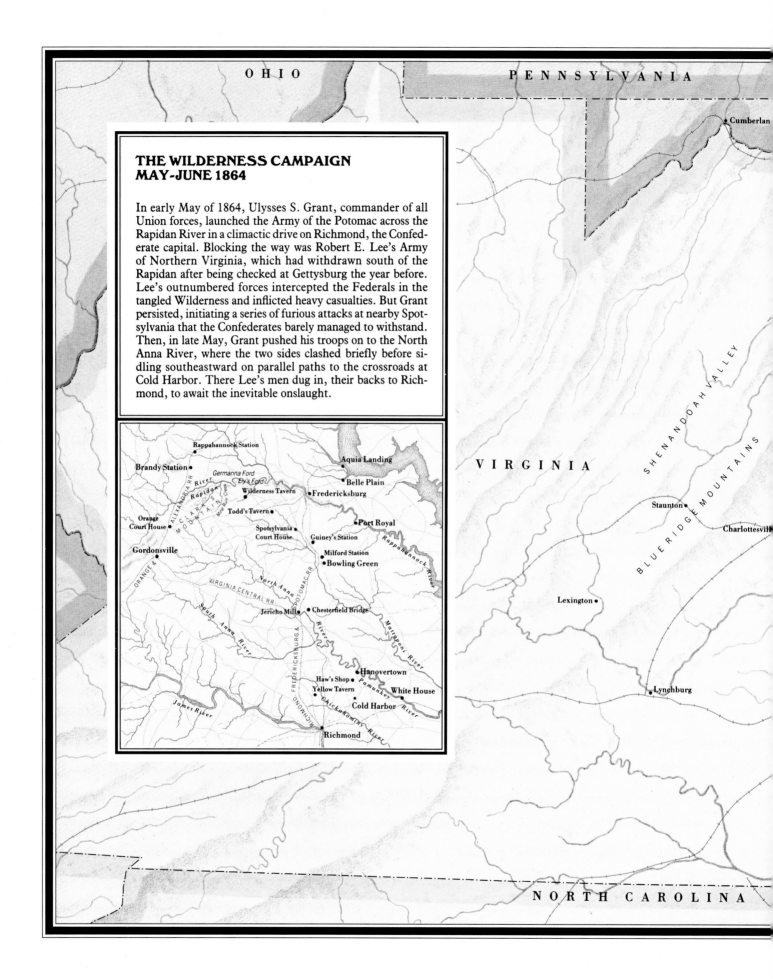

OHIO   PENNSYLVANIA

Cumberlan

THE WILDERNESS CAMPAIGN
MAY-JUNE 1864

In early May of 1864, Ulysses S. Grant, commander of all
Union forces, launched the Army of the Potomac across the
Rapidan River in a climactic drive on Richmond, the Confed-
erate capital. Blocking the way was Robert E. Lee's Army
of Northern Virginia, which had withdrawn south of the
Rapidan after being checked at Gettysburg the year before.
Lee's outnumbered forces intercepted the Federals in the
tangled Wilderness and inflicted heavy casualties. But Grant
persisted, initiating a series of furious attacks at nearby Spotsylvania that the Confederates barely managed to withstand.
Then, in late May, Grant pushed his troops on to the North
Anna River, where the two sides clashed briefly before sidling southeastward on parallel paths to the crossroads at
Cold Harbor. There Lee's men dug in, their backs to Richmond, to await the inevitable onslaught.

VIRGINIA

SHENANDOAH VALLEY

BLUE RIDGE MOUNTAINS

Staunton

Charlottesvill

Lexington

Lynchburg

Rappahannock Station

Brandy Station

Germanna Ford
Ely's Ford
Wilderness Tavern   Aquia Landing

Belle Plain

Fredericksburg

Todd's Tavern

Orange
Court House   Port Royal

Spotsylvania
Court House   Guiney's Station

Gordonsville   Milford Station
Bowling Green

North Anna   Rappahannock River

VIRGINIA CENTRAL R.R.

Jericho Mill   Chesterfield Bridge

South Anna River   Mattaponi River

James River   Hanovertown

Haw's Shop   Pamunkey River
Yellow Tavern   White House

Chickahominy River   Cold Harbor

Richmond

NORTH CAROLINA

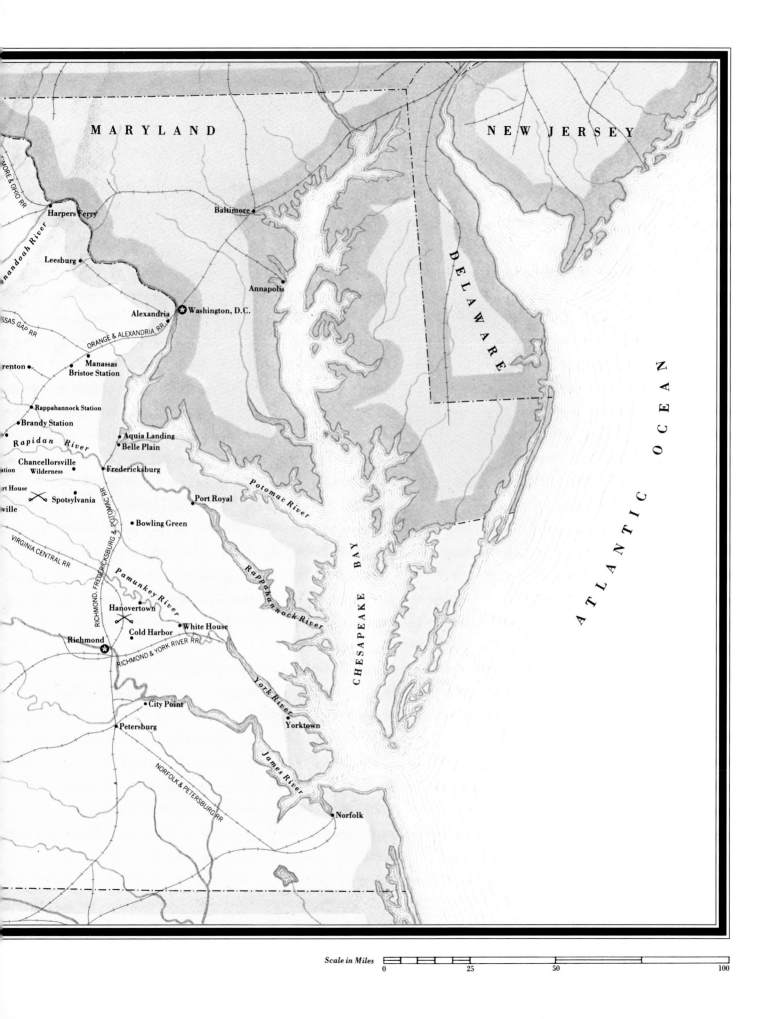

MARYLAND

NEW JERSEY

DELAWARE

BALTIMORE & OHIO RR

Shenandoah River

Harpers Ferry

Leesburg

MANASSAS GAP RR

Alexandria

ORANGE & ALEXANDRIA RR

Washington, D.C.

Baltimore

Annapolis

renton

Manassas
Bristoe Station

Rappahannock Station

Brandy Station

Rapidan River

Chancellorsville
Wilderness
ation

rt House

ville

Spotsylvania

Aquia Landing
Belle Plain

Fredericksburg

Port Royal

Potomac River

VIRGINIA CENTRAL RR

Bowling Green

RICHMOND, FREDERICKSBURG & POTOMAC RR

Pamunkey River

Hanovertown

Cold Harbor   White House

Richmond

RICHMOND & YORK RIVER RR

Rappahannock River

CHESAPEAKE BAY

York River

City Point

Petersburg

Yorktown

NORFOLK & PETERSBURG RR

James River

Norfolk

ATLANTIC OCEAN

Scale in Miles

0   25   50   100

Other Publications:

UNDERSTANDING COMPUTERS
YOUR HOME
THE ENCHANTED WORLD
THE KODAK LIBRARY OF CREATIVE PHOTOGRAPHY
GREAT MEALS IN MINUTES
PLANET EARTH
COLLECTOR'S LIBRARY OF THE CIVIL WAR
THE EPIC OF FLIGHT
THE GOOD COOK
WORLD WAR II
HOME REPAIR AND IMPROVEMENT
THE OLD WEST

For information on and a full description of any of the
Time-Life Books series listed above, please write:
Reader Information, Time-Life Books
541 North Fairbanks Court, Chicago, Illinois 60611

This volume is one of a series that chronicles in full the
events of the American Civil War, 1861-1865.
Other books in the series include:
Brother against Brother: The War Begins
First Blood: Fort Sumter to Bull Run
The Blockade: Runners and Raiders
The Road to Shiloh: Early Battles in the West
Forward to Richmond: McClellan's Peninsular Campaign
Decoying the Yanks: Jackson's Valley Campaign
Confederate Ordeal: The Southern Home Front
Lee Takes Command: From Seven Days to Second Bull Run
The Coastal War: Chesapeake Bay to Rio Grande
Tenting Tonight: The Soldier's Life
The Bloodiest Day: The Battle of Antietam
War on the Mississippi: Grant's Vicksburg Campaign
Rebels Resurgent: Fredericksburg to Chancellorsville
Twenty Million Yankees: The Northern Home Front
Gettysburg: The Confederate High Tide
The Struggle for Tennessee: Tupelo to Stones River
The Fight for Chattanooga: Chickamauga to Missionary Ridge
Spies, Scouts and Raiders: Irregular Operations
The Battles for Atlanta: Sherman Moves East

The Cover: Attacking near Spotsylvania Court
House early on May 12, 1864, Federals of Winfield Scott Hancock's corps surge over breastworks with bayonets fixed to grapple with Confederates defending a salient known thereafter as
the Bloody Angle. Each side suffered more than
6,000 casualties that day in a contest that epito-
mized Ulysses S. Grant's relentless campaign to crush
Robert E. Lee's army and take Richmond.

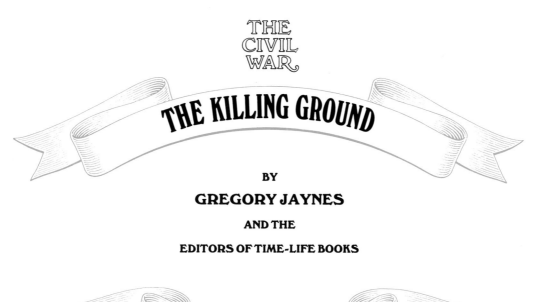

THE
CIVIL
WAR

THE KILLING GROUND

BY

GREGORY JAYNES

AND THE

EDITORS OF TIME-LIFE BOOKS

Wilderness to Cold Harbor

TIME-LIFE BOOKS, ALEXANDRIA, VIRGINIA

Time-Life Books Inc.
is a wholly owned subsidiary of
TIME INCORPORATED

FOUNDER: Henry R. Luce 1898-1967

Editor-in-Chief: Henry Anatole Grunwald
President: J. Richard Munro
Chairman of the Board: Ralph P. Davidson
Corporate Editor: Ray Cave
Group Vice President, Books: Reginald K. Brack Jr.
Vice President, Books: George Artandi

TIME-LIFE BOOKS INC.

EDITOR: George Constable
Executive Editor: George Daniels
Editorial General Manager: Neal Goff
Director of Design: Louis Klein
Director of Editorial Resources: Phyllis K. Wise
Editorial Board: Dale M. Brown, Roberta Conlan,
Ellen Phillips, Donia Ann Steele, Rosalind Stubenberg,
Kit van Tulleken, Henry Woodhead
Director of Research and Photography:
John Conrad Weiser

PRESIDENT: Reginald K. Brack Jr.
Executive Vice Presidents: John M. Fahey Jr.,
Christopher T. Linen
Senior Vice President: James L. Mercer
Vice Presidents: Stephen L. Bair, Edward Brash,
Ralph J. Cuomo, Juanita T. James, Wilhelm R. Saake,
Robert H. Smith, Paul R. Stewart, Leopoldo Toralballa

The Civil War
Series Director: Henry Woodhead
Designer: Edward Frank
Series Administrator: Philip Brandt George

Editorial Staff for *The Killing Ground*
Associate Editors: Thomas H. Flaherty Jr.,
David S. Thomson (text); Jane Coughran (pictures)
Staff Writers: R. W. Murphy, Daniel Stashower
Researchers: Patti H. Cass, Brian C. Pohanka
(principals); Harris J. Andrews, Kristin Baker
Copy Coordinator: Jayne E. Rohrich
Picture Coordinator: Betty H. Weatherley
Editorial Assistant: Donna Fountain
Special Contributor: Brian McGinn

Editorial Operations
Copy Chief: Diane Ullius
Editorial Operations: Caroline A. Boubin (manager)
Production: Celia Beattie
Quality Control: James J. Cox (director)
Library: Louise D. Forstall

Correspondents: Elisabeth Kraemer-Singh (Bonn);
Dorothy Bacon (London); Maria Vincenza Aloisi,
Josephine du Brusle (Paris); Ann Natanson (Rome).
Valuable assistance was also provided by: Carolyn
Chubet (New York).

The Author:
Gregory Jaynes is a former foreign and national correspondent for *The New York Times.* Since 1983 he has contributed the "American Scene" column to *Time* from his home in Atlanta, Georgia.

The Consultants:
Colonel John R. Elting, USA (Ret.), a former Associate Professor at West Point, is the author of *Battles for Scandinavia* in the Time-Life Books World War II series and of *The Battle of Bunker's Hill, The Battles of Saratoga, Military History and Atlas of the Napoleonic Wars, American Army Life* and *The Superstrategists.* Co-author of *A Dictionary of Soldier Talk,* he is also editor of the three volumes of *Military Uniforms in America, 1755-1867,* and associate editor of *The West Point Atlas of American Wars.*

William A. Frassanito, a Civil War historian and lecturer specializing in photograph analysis, is the author of two award-winning studies, *Gettysburg: A Journey in Time* and *Antietam: The Photographic Legacy of America's Bloodiest Day,* and a companion volume, *Grant and Lee, The Virginia Campaigns.* He has also served as chief consultant to the photographic history series *The Image of War.*

Les Jensen, Director of the Second Armored Division Museum, Fort Hood, Texas, specializes in Civil War artifacts and is a conservator of historic flags. He is a contributor to *The Image of War* series, consultant for numerous Civil War publications and museums, and a member of the Company of Military Historians. He was formerly Curator of the U.S. Army Transportation Museum at Fort Eustis, Virginia, and before that Curator of the Museum of the Confederacy in Richmond, Virginia.

Michael McAfee specializes in military uniforms and has been Curator of Uniforms and History at the West Point Museum since 1970. A fellow of the Company of Military Historians, he coedited with Colonel Elting *Long Endure: The Civil War Years,* and he collaborated with Frederick Todd on *American Military Equipage.* He is the author of *Artillery of the American Revolution, 1775-1783,* and has written numerous articles for *Military Images Magazine.*

James P. Shenton, Professor of History at Columbia University, is a specialist in 19th-century American political and social history, with particular emphasis on the Civil War period. He is the author of *Robert John Walker* and *Reconstruction South.*

Library of Congress Cataloguing in Publication Data
Jaynes, Gregory.
    The killing ground.
    (The Civil War)
    Bibliography: p.
    Includes index.
    1. Virginia — History — Civil War, 1861-1865 —
Campaigns.   2. Wilderness, Battle of the, 1864.
3. Spotsylvania, Battle of, 1864.   4. Cold Harbor,
Battle of, 1864.   5. Petersburg (Va.) — History —
Siege, 1864.   I. Time-Life Books.   II. Title.
III. Series.
E470.2.J39 1986   973.7'36   86-1256
ISBN 0-8094-4768-1
ISBN 0-8094-4769-X (lib. bdg.)

CONTENTS

Wintering Over at Brandy Station

In November of 1863 General George Meade's Army of the Potomac withdrew into winter quarters for a season of watching and waiting. All that separated Meade's forces from those of Robert E. Lee was the narrow Rapidan River, "the passing of which by either army," wrote a Federal soldier, "would be the signal for battle."

That signal would not come for more than five months. In the interim, the Federal army established a winter city of more than 100,000 men, the largest encampment of the War. Centered on Brandy Station, it stretched over an area 10 miles square. The Union could hardly have chosen a less agreeable spot. The scene of fierce fighting during the summer, the countryside was one "broad expanse of pap," wrote one offi-

The camp of the 18th Pennsylvania Cavalry boasts a long row of log huts, many with barrel chimneys, and corduroy platforms to keep the horses' hoofs out of the mu

cer, "ornamented with stumps, dead horses and mules, deserted camps and thousands upon thousands of crows." Another officer added, "*Mud, mud*, is the order of the day here. Splash, splash, we go all day."

Despite the dreary terrain, the encampment itself was remarkably comfortable. The men lived in huts and tents warmed by wood fires and enjoyed amenities that were seldom available in the field. Through the winter the camp was alive with a constant flow of visitors, including, as one officer jokingly noted, "perfect shoals of womenkind." The men were also cheered by the arrival of Lieutenant General Ulysses S. Grant, the commander in chief of the Federal armies. Grant was a known fighter with a proven record, and he brought with him the promise of decisive action in the spring. Few of the soldiers could have predicted just how costly that action would be, but when the April thaw came they seemed in good shape to fight. "They had been drilling hard all winter and showed it," Captain George Sanford wrote. "They were trim and as hard as nails" — ready to cross the Rapidan and take the war to Robert E. Lee.

hen the animals were tied up. The huts were drier and more hospitable than tents, even though, as one soldier put it, they had "few claims to architectural beauty."

Captain George Meade Jr. *(third from left)* dines with fellow officers of his father's staff at Brandy Station in April of 1864. That same month, Colonel Theodore Lyman *(second from right)* wrote to his wife of the peaceful springtime: "I suppose we may call this the lull before the hurricane, which little short of a miracle can avert."

General Meade *(fourth from right)* visits the staff of 1st Brigade's Horse Artillery at its headquarters; such impromptu reviews were dreaded by Meade's men. He was known for his irascible disposition and could be, according to one staff member, "like a firework, always going bang at someone, and nobody ever knows who is going to catch it next, but all stand in a semi-terrified state."

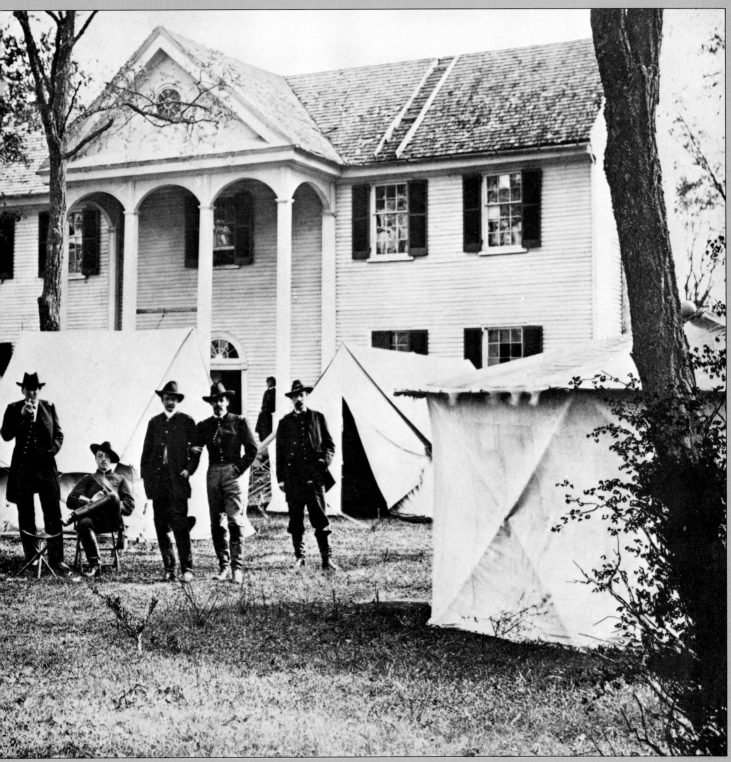

General Meade's aides gather in front of Wallach house, which served as the army's headquarters at the winter encampment. Seated at left are Captain Frederick Rosencrantz (*fourth from left*) — a Swede known as "Old Rosey" to his fellows — and Major James Biddle (*third from left*), a clownish officer of whom it was once remarked, "If there is a wrong road, he's sure to take it."

Officers of General John Sedgwick's staff pose languidly before a log cabin. Third from left is General George McClellan's brother, Arthur, a captain. At far left is Lieutenant Colonel Thomas Hyde, who wrote of camp life: "Reviews, balls, races, and the mail from home were the joyful incidents that dispelled monotony."

A group of provost marshal clerks gathers beside a wall tent that is coupled with a tall Sibley tent. The protruding stovepipe suggests that the arrangement provided a warm and comfortable gathering place during the cold winter months.

While one officer stands by, two others entertain female visitors in front of their tent, which has been erected adjacent to an old chimney. Foliage of pine, cedar and holly has been collected and woven into garlands to beautify the quarters.

Staff of the U.S. Sanitary Commission pose for a photograph at their Brandy Station headquarters, a place made neat and tidy by the addition of a picket fence, a stone wall and a footbridge. The commission, a private relief agency, worked to raise the hygienic standards in camp and to provide extra food and clothing for the soldiers.

The mail wagon of II Corps stands ready to make its appointed rounds. Each Army corps at Brandy Station had its own mail service to handle the voluminous correspondence between the soldiers and their loved ones in the North.

Customers gather around the tent of sutler A. Foulke, who sold tobacco, candy, canned goods, stationery and, occasionally, whiskey. Sutlers were under strict orders not to sell any spirits to enlisted men, but enterprising soldiers sometimes donned shoulder straps to impersonate officers and wrangle whiskey.

The ammunition train of the Cavalry Corps's 3rd Division rolls into camp, bringing supplies from the North. The winter lull in the fighting gave Meade's army an opportunity to build up its stores of weapons and ammunition for the coming campaign.

Quartermasters of General John Sedgwick's VI Corps lean against the railing of a wooden walkway in front of the ambulance camp at Hazel River, near Brandy Station. During the winter months, when there were few injured men to transport, ambulances were mostly used to ferry men and supplies across the encampment.

Rows of barrels and stacks of crates sit at trackside, awaiting distribution by Union quartermasters. The group of buildings along the tracks in the background is Brandy Station itself, nucleus of the encampment.

A pontoon boat, one of many assembled at Brandy Station, sits in its carriage awaiting the effort to bridge the Rapidan River. In the coming offensive, Meade's engineers would throw five pontoon spans across the Rapidan in less than two hours.

Carpenters, wheelwrights and harness makers bend to their tasks at the army repair shop of IX Corps, building and mending army wagons. An observer was deeply impressed with how "the lusty artificers of the corps carry on their needful trades, doing much good work."

In this Union wagon park stand 240 of the 6,000 wagons that would follow Grant's troops across the Rapidan River in the offensive against Robert E. I

The 17th Maine, a regiment of 507 men, drills on a field at Brandy Station on May 3, 1864, the day before the unit marched into

uring the Federal army's advance, the Union supply train stretched for 60 miles.

derness. Within four days, 192 of these men would be battle casualties, including 54 dead.

Grant Takes Charge

"The feeling about Grant is peculiar — a little jealousy, a little dislike, a little envy, a little want of confidence — only brilliant success will dissipate the elements. If he succeeds, the war is over. For I do assure you that in the hands of a General who gave them success, there is no force on earth which would resist this Army."

CAPTAIN CHARLES FRANCIS ADAMS JR., 1ST MASSACHUSETTS CAVALRY

1

General Ulysses S. Grant was at his winter headquarters in Nashville on March 3, 1864, when he received word from Edwin Stanton, the Secretary of War, that he was to assume command of all the Union armies. Five days later Grant reached Washington with his eldest son, Fred, in tow. Through a mixup, no one met their train, and when the rumpled officer and the 13-year-old boy presented themselves at the desk of Willard's Hotel, the clerk was less than impressed. The conqueror of Vicksburg and Chattanooga signed the register simply "U. S. Grant and Son, Galena, Illinois."

The name worked instant magic. Grant's victories in the West had made him the most talked about man in the Union. Indeed, the New York *Herald* for months had been promoting him as a grassroots candidate for President in the forthcoming election. The desk clerk, recovering nicely, immediately assigned Grant the best suite in the house — the one where Lincoln had stayed before his inauguration. The clientele in the lobby of Willard's, a room of "heat, noise, dust, smoke and expectoration" according to a visitor, quickly got word of Grant's presence and began to measure the man.

At five feet eight inches tall and 135 pounds, there was not much on the outside to measure. The distinguished writer Richard Henry Dana Jr., encountering Grant at the Willard a bit later, described him as an "ordinary, scrubby looking man with a slightly seedy look, as if he was out of office on half pay; he had no gait, no station, no manner." Even Dana conceded, however, that the 41-year-old general had a certain "look of resolution, as if he could not be trifled with."

For Grant, the intense public scrutiny was only beginning. Later in the day he learned that he was expected at the White House that evening, a Tuesday, when President and Mrs. Lincoln held their weekly reception.

Grant walked the two blocks to the White House, where the President was greeting guests in the Blue Room. The two men from Illinois had never met, but Lincoln recognized his visitor from across the room and stepped forward to pump his hand. "Why, here is General Grant!" exclaimed the President, who towered eight inches above his guest. "Well, this is a great pleasure, I assure you." Lincoln's pleasure was much more than social. After three years of searching, he suspected he had found a general.

In Grant, Lincoln perceived a military leader who would make up for the failures of the past. Lincoln's field commanders in the East had fallen short of the mark. A succession of men of promise — George McClellan, Ambrose Burnside, Joseph Hooker and now George Meade — had failed to score the decisive victory and bring the Confederacy to its knees. Even after Gettysburg, a defeat for

Ulysses S. Grant, more concerned with comfort than appearance, is shown wearing his lieutenant general's uniform with his usual casual air.

the Confederacy, General Meade had allowed Robert E. Lee's Army of Northern Virginia to slip away — and in eight months of maneuvering had not struck Lee a killing blow. Lincoln now was placing the hopes of the Union squarely on the shoulders of the man from Illinois. The President's judgment would be put to the test that spring as his new commander led the Army of the Potomac against the forces of Lee in a series of battles whose names would live in history: the Wilderness, Spotsylvania and Cold Harbor.

At the White House, Grant was ushered into the East Room, where most of official Washington, it seemed, was straining for a glimpse of the heralded newcomer. At Grant's entrance, the crowd's enthusiasm boiled over. Men and women surged forward to cheer him and shake his hand. Secretary of the Navy Gideon Welles, looking on with distaste, thought the scene "rowdy and unseemly." A reporter present wrote that "it was the only real mob I ever saw at the White House."

When someone in the crowd cried out, "Stand up, so we can all have a look at you!" Grant obliged by climbing onto a sofa. He remained there, accepting the adulation, for almost an hour. "For once, at least, the President of the United States was not the chief figure in the picture," a journalist recorded. "The little, scared-looking man who stood on the crimson-colored sofa was the idol of the hour."

The following afternoon Grant returned to the White House to receive the commission of lieutenant general in a formal ceremony. It was the loftiest rank his government had to bestow; the Union had major generals by the score, but before Grant, only George

Washington and Winfield Scott had risen to lieutenant general, and Scott's rank was by brevet, or honorary. Grant read his acceptance in a loud, clear voice. "I feel the full weight of the responsibilities now devolving on me," he declared, "and it will be my earnest endeavor not to disappoint your expectations."

When his brief speech was over, Grant accepted the evidently sincere congratulations of the man he was replacing as general in chief, Henry Halleck. Grant wisely agreed with his trusted subordinate, William Tecumseh Sherman, who had told him bluntly, "Halleck is better qualified than you to stand the buffets of intrigue and policy." Halleck would assume a new title, chief of staff — the "office man," as one of Grant's staff officers called him. He would continue to shoulder the administrative chores of running the Army, thus sparing Grant that burden.

Assured that his duties in Washington had been fulfilled, Grant had one more sensitive matter to dispose of. On March 10 he traveled the 60 miles to Brandy Station, Virginia, where the Army of the Potomac had its headquarters, to meet with that army's commander, Major General George Meade. The patrician Meade, seven years Grant's senior, knew that his job was in danger because of his failure to bring Lee to bay. Earlier, Grant had contemplated replacing Meade with one of his own generals from the West — either Sherman or William F. (Baldy) Smith. Meade, like George McClellan, it seemed, was unwilling to take the risks that might lead to ultimate victory.

But now Grant's plans were changing. Meade, a somber man with great bags under his eyes, was known for his temper-fired tongue, but he greeted Grant warmly at

President Lincoln and General Grant *(right of center)* meet for the first time at a White House reception on March 8, 1864. The artist was so eager to include portraits of the military heroes of the day that he let his imagination triumph over fact. Generals Sherman, Meade and McClellan are shown standing in a cluster to the left and Winfield Scott sits among the ladies at right; in reality none of the four were present.

Brandy Station. Moreover, he immediately disarmed Grant by offering to step down. Meade urged Grant not to hesitate because of concern for Meade's pride. "The work before us is of such vast importance to the whole nation," Meade said, "that the feelings or wishes of no one person should stand in the way of selecting the right men for all positions."

Grant liked Meade's forthrightness and told him he had "no thought of substituting anyone" for him. A week later Meade wrote his wife, "I was much pleased with Grant." He added, "You may rest assured he is not an ordinary man."

Nor was Grant going to be an ordinary commander. On March 17 he issued General Order No. 1, which began: "I assume command of the Armies of the United States, headquarters in the field, and until notice these will be those of the Army of the Po-

tomac." Meade would continue to lead the fight against Lee, but Grant would map the way — not from Washington or from the West (as Sherman had repeatedly urged him), but from a tent not far from Meade's.

Now Grant took a train west to meet with Sherman, whom he had named as his replacement in command of the Union's Western armies; with Sherman, Grant would plan a grand strategy for defeating the Confederacy. The two men took rooms in a Cincinnati hotel and consulted their maps. As Grant later wrote in his memoirs, the maps showed that in March of 1864 the Union held: the Mississippi River, from St. Louis south to the Gulf of Mexico; the mouth of the Rio Grande; nearly all of the state of Tennessee, from Memphis to Chattanooga; West Virginia; and that part of Virginia north of the Rapidan River. The Union also held the Virginia seaport of Norfolk as well as Fort Monroe; the North Carolina ports of Plymouth, Washington and New Bern; the South Carolina coastal town of Beaufort, and Hilton Head, Folly and Morris Islands; and in Florida the Federals possessed Fernandina, St. Augustine, Pensacola and Key West. Nevertheless, Grant characterized that part of the South still in Confederate control as "an empire in extent."

To defeat this empire, Grant had under his command about 662,000 soldiers, organized in 22 corps. Of these men, probably 533,000 were combat-ready effectives—the largest host any American officer had ever commanded. Grant's plan of action was uncomplicated but unique to the Civil War. He intended to put all his armies on the move that spring in simultaneous, concerted offensives that would exhaust the enemy and destroy the Confederacy's logistical capacity to continue the War. Grant's primary objective was not to occupy territory, but to conquer the two strong armies the South still had in the field: Lee's forces in Virginia and the consolidated Western army now commanded by General Joseph E. Johnston.

Sherman's army of 100,000 troops was stationed in northwest Georgia, just below Chattanooga. Between Sherman and Atlanta lay Johnston's Confederate force. Sherman later concisely summarized his Cincinnati meeting with Grant: "He was to go for Lee and I was to go for Joe Johnston. That was the plan."

When Grant returned to the East, he issued succinct orders to Meade: "Lee's army will be your objective point. Wherever Lee goes, there you will go also." Grant also planned to put two additional Federal armies on the move in Virginia. Major General Franz Sigel had 26,000 men spread over northern Maryland and West Virginia, covering primarily the Baltimore & Ohio Railroad. Grant ordered Sigel to drive south through the Shenandoah Valley to deprive Lee of food and rail support from that quarter. Grant's other army in Virginia, under Major General Benjamin Butler, was concentrated on the Peninsula, between the York and James Rivers. Grant informed Butler that his ultimate objective was to be the Confederate capital of Richmond. Butler was to advance up the south bank of the James River with 30,000 men to City Point, just south of Petersburg. There he was to fortify his position and look for an opportunity to join Meade's Army of the Potomac in a massive pincers movement.

Grant's foe, Robert E. Lee, had endured a long season of frustration. The campaigns of 1863 had cost his Army of Northern Virginia dearly, especially in officers. These were losses that the South, with its smaller population, could not replace.

Beaten at Gettysburg, Lee had retreated slowly up the Shenandoah Valley. A rash of desertions had further sapped the army's strength, and Lee's grim resort to the firing squad did not help morale. Lee offered to resign his command, an offer immediately refused by President Jefferson Davis.

To the east of Lee, General Meade had sidestepped southward from Pennsylvania, keeping his army between the Confederates and Washington at all times. Though prudent, Meade's performance earned a withering rebuke from Lincoln, who said it reminded him "of an old woman trying to shoo her geese across a creek."

Lee's retreat ended south of the Rappahannock River in late July 1863, and in the

The commission at right, certify his promotion to the rank of li tenant general, was presente U. S. Grant at a White House tion on March 9, 1864. Grant alm did not live to attend the ceremo the night before, as he sat for a p trait in Mathew Brady's photograp studio, a glass skylight collaps nearly killing the gene

Recorded Volume 1, Page 185
Adjutant General's Office
March 4th 1864
W. A. Nichols
Asst. Adjt. Genl.

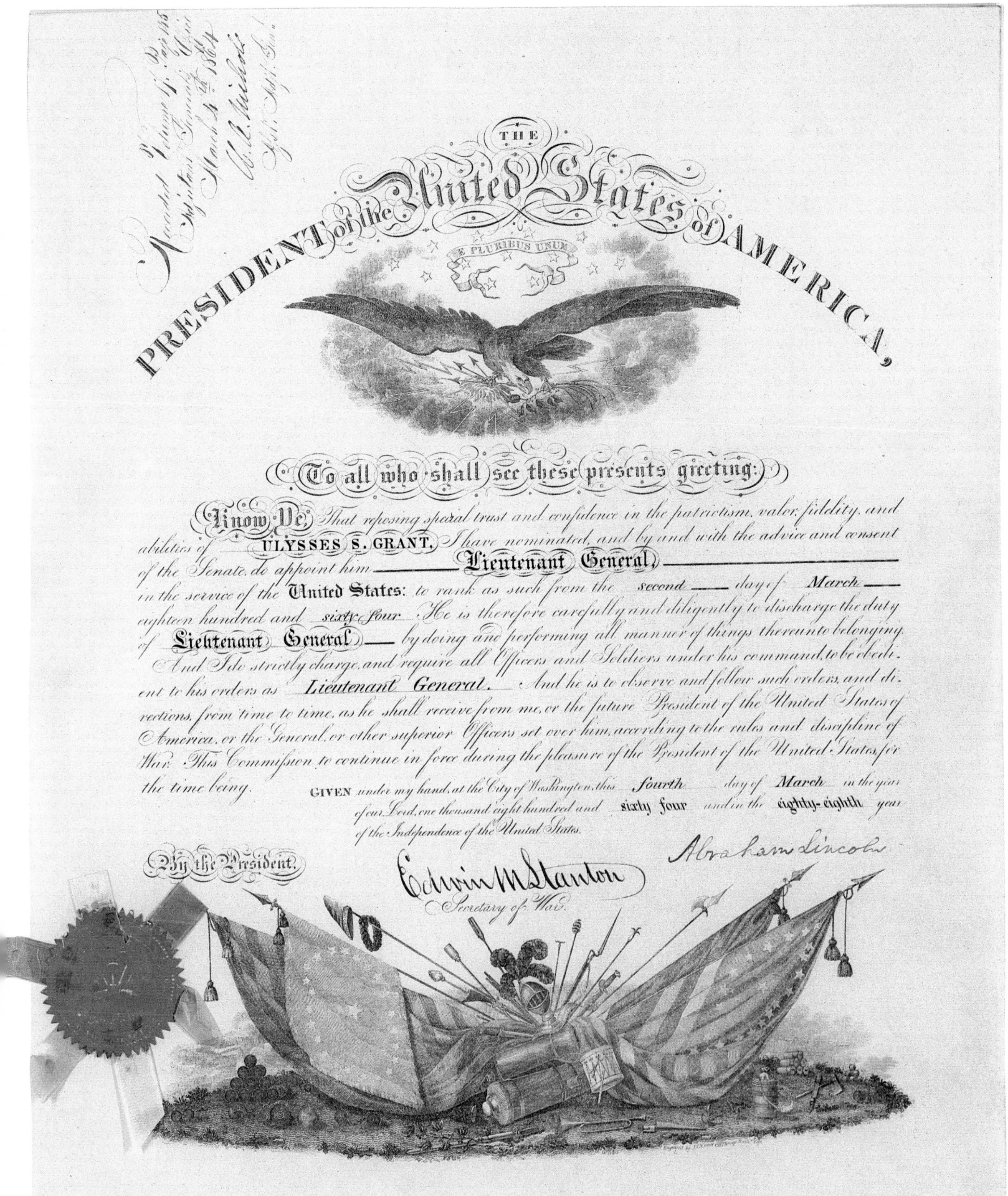

THE PRESIDENT of the United States of AMERICA,

E PLURIBUS UNUM

To all who shall see these presents greeting:

Know Ye, That reposing special trust and confidence in the patriotism, valor, fidelity, and abilities of ULYSSES S. GRANT, I have nominated, and by and with the advice and consent of the Senate, do appoint him Lieutenant General, in the service of the United States: to rank as such from the second day of March eighteen hundred and sixty four. He is therefore carefully and diligently to discharge the duty of Lieutenant General by doing and performing all manner of things thereunto belonging.

And I do strictly charge and require all Officers and Soldiers under his command, to be obedient to his orders as Lieutenant General. And he is to observe and follow such orders, and directions, from time to time, as he shall receive from me, or the future President of the United States of America, or the General, or other superior Officers set over him, according to the rules and discipline of War. This Commission to continue in force during the pleasure of the President of the United States for the time being.

GIVEN under my hand, at the City of Washington, this fourth day of March in the year of our Lord, one thousand eight hundred and sixty four and in the eighty-eighth year of the Independence of the United States.

Abraham Lincoln

By the President.

Edwin M Stanton
Secretary of War.

ensuing months the rival armies engaged in a campaign of maneuver — marching much, fighting little. Both armies were temporarily reduced by appeals from the West for reinforcement. Lee dispatched two divisions under his ablest commander, Lieutenant General James Longstreet, to Tennessee. When Meade discovered that Lee's army had been weakened by Longstreet's departure, he launched an advance that pushed the Confederates south of the Rapidan. But then Meade was compelled to send two corps of his own to Tennessee to counter Longstreet's arrival there.

Now it was Lee's turn to take advantage of the weakened Army of the Potomac. In early October, after learning that XI and XII Corps had left for the West, Lee swung his forces around Cedar Mountain and marched northeast in an attempt to turn Meade's right flank. Meade responded with skill, however, retreating smoothly along the Orange & Alexandria Railroad to Manassas and beyond.

When Lee's III Corps under Lieutenant General A. P. Hill caught up with Meade's rear guard at Bristoe Station, just south of Manassas, the Confederates charged headlong into an ambush and were shattered, losing 1,900 men. Lee pulled back to the south bank of the Rapidan — methodically destroying the railroad as his only solace — and his men began building huts for shelter against the oncoming winter.

But Meade, singed by criticism from Washington, was not through for the season. On November 21 he received an intelligence report indicating that Lee's army was only half the size of his. (In fact, Meade had 81,000 men to Lee's 48,000.) Buoyed by the report, Meade planned a flanking attack across the Rapidan. Lee's two corps — Hill's and a second commanded by Lieutenant General Richard Ewell — were strung out on a line 35 miles long stretching from the river southwest to Orange Court House. Meade intended to march his five corps swiftly

The crutches and empty sleeves of these Confederate prisoners at Gettysburg's Camp Letterman General Hospital attest to the reduced strength of Lee's army. By the end of the Gettysburg Campaign, more than a third of the 75,000 Confederates engaged were dead, wounded, captured or missing — losses the South could no longer replace.

downstream, ford the Rapidan, and knife between Ewell's and Hill's corps, destroying each one separately.

Federal infantry commanders got their orders to march half an hour before sunrise on November 26, Thanksgiving Day. No supply trains would slow the advance; each man would carry 10 days' rations instead.

But Lee was watchful. On the 24th, after learning from a scout that Meade had called up large quantities of rations, Lee alerted his outposts. The next day Confederate cavalry clashed with advancing Federal troopers near Ely's Ford. And when the Confederate signal station on Clark's Mountain spotted the movement of the Federal infantry and ordnance wagons early on the 26th, Lee started to shift his forces. He ordered Major General Jubal Early, who had temporarily replaced the ailing Richard Ewell, to withdraw II Corps quickly from its fortifications along the Rapidan River and march westward to meet the threat. The rest of the army would follow.

Meade was about to be foiled again. He had assigned III Corps, under Major General William French, to lead the advance. French's troops got a late start—with dire consequences. Major General John Sedgwick's VI Corps, which was to follow in French's path, stepped off at sunrise but soon found itself bottled up in French's occupied camps. French's troops "should have been out of camp before we arrived," wrote George T. Stevens, a surgeon in the 77th New York, "but as yet not a tent was struck nor a wagon loaded, and most of the men were asleep in their quarters. The VI Corps was obliged to halt and stand in the mud for hours, waiting for the delinquent corps to get out of the way."

The confusion did not end there. Once across the river, French's corps took the wrong road and led the army in the wrong direction. Once the Federals got on track, ankle-deep mud and cold rain slowed their advance. There were other frustrations. An engineering unit miscalculated the Rapidan's width and built a pontoon bridge that fell one pontoon short of the far bank.

The mistakes cost the Federals a day's time and gave Lee an extended opportunity to prepare. On November 27 Meade had all five of his infantry corps and one cavalry corps south of the Rapidan, advancing westward. In the lead on the Federal left flank was II Corps, temporarily under the command of Major General Gouverneur Kemble Warren. As Warren's lead elements passed through the settlement of Locust Grove, they collided with Brigadier General Harry Hays's division. Both sides entrenched and a standoff ensued. At 4 p.m. French's troops moved up on Warren's right flank and ran into a Confederate division commanded by Major General Edward Johnson.

Although Johnson's veterans were outnumbered 3 to 1, they attacked. Brigadier General George H. Steuart launched his brigade against French's right flank. One of Steuart's regimental commanders, Lieutenant Colonel Simeon T. Walton of the 23rd Virginia, was quickly wounded but refused to leave his men. As the Confederates swept forward, they were suddenly rocked by canister fire from two Federal batteries. Steuart's troops faltered, then turned back, leaving behind them 170 casualties. Among the fallen was the gallant Walton, shot through the head.

To Steuart's right, three of Johnson's brigades charged across a field on Payne's farm,

In early October of 1863, when Lee's flanking maneuver forced a temporary Federal retreat from Culpeper, photographer A. J. Russell was on hand to record the withdrawal. What began as a routine series of photographs of a cavalry unit (*below, left*) and commissary wagons (*below, right*) took a dramatic turn when the marching orders came. A winter hut is set aflame as trains are hastily loaded (*bottom left*) and soldiers perch on top of railcars as they are pulled from the station (*bottom right*).

cheering as they ran. From the cover of dense brush on the other side of the field, two Federal divisions leveled a withering fire. The Confederates were staggered and they paused in confusion. Brigadier General James A. Walker, commander of the Stonewall Brigade, feared that his men might break and spurred his horse forward. He grabbed the flag of one of his regiments, leaped his horse over a fence, rode into the field and rallied his troops. With a cheer, they rushed on.

But it was all for nothing. The Confederates were stymied by the thickets from which the Federals were firing. "It was found impossible to maintain an unbroken line," General Johnson reported, "and each brigade commander, in turn, finding himself unsupported either on the right or the left, ordered back his brigade."

The Confederates had been halted, but they had punished the Federals. When the firing stopped at dusk, French had lost 950 men to Johnson's 545. And Johnson's attack proved costly to the Federals in another way — it convinced French that he faced overwhelming odds and riveted him in place. French's inaction gave Lee sufficient time to move his forces to a ridge behind a creek known as Mine Run, which ran due north and emptied into the Rapidan.

The next day, Union scouts, cautiously probing westward, encountered Mine Run; beyond the creek they could see what one of Meade's soldiers called a "a very ugly looking line of hills, rendered more repulsive in aspect by fallen trees and lines of freshly dug earth." Atop the hills stood an array of "infantry parapets, abatis, and epaulements for batteries."

Lee waited behind his seven-mile-long line for Meade to attack. For two days Meade probed and entrenched; the weather was so wet and cold that his pickets had to be relieved every half hour in order to keep them from freezing. One Federal recalled that "though our drooping eyelids called pitifully for sleep, each soldier knew that to sleep uncovered in that bitter air would be the sleep of death."

Many Union soldiers prepared for the impending battle by writing their names and regiments on slips of paper so they could be identified if killed. A few grimly added the words "killed in action, November 30, 1863." On that day, Meade planned to attack. Warren's II Corps would launch the offensive, and all of the other corps were to key their attacks on the sound of Warren's gunfire. But Warren, whose judgment had been so crucial to Federal success on the second day of the Battle of Gettysburg, was appalled by the formidable Confederate earthworks lined with troops and bristling with artillery. He decided that an attack would be suicidal, and on his own initiative he called off the assault. "The works cannot be taken," he told Meade. "I would sooner sacrifice my commission than my men." Meade, although infuriated by Warren's insubordination, reluctantly agreed with him and abandoned the offensive.

Lee now determined to launch a flank attack on Warren's left, but on December 2, when Confederate troops ventured forth, they found nothing but air. The Union columns had already begun retracing their steps across the Rapidan.

Meade sensed that he was courting "certain personal ruin" by not attacking, for he was convinced that his critics believed it "would be better to strew the road to Richmond with the dead bodies of our soldiers than that there should be nothing done." He assumed that he would soon be replaced. In this, Meade was wrong; but the retreat from Mine Run was virtually his last independent command decision.

The Army of the Potomac settled into winter quarters above the Rapidan, around Culpeper and Brandy Station. Life on the north bank of the river, according to a homesick Federal colonel, was "miserably lazy. Hardly an order to carry, and the horses all eating their heads off. If one could only be at home, till one was *wanted*, and then be on the spot. But this is everywhere the way of war; lie still and lie still; then up and maneuver and march hard; then a big battle; and then a lot more lie still."

Nor was the pace on the south bank any different. "We had little to do," wrote Captain James F. J. Caldwell of the 1st South Carolina. "The weather did not admit of much drilling, nor of regular guard duty, so that picket was the only military exercise constantly required of us."

As they had in previous winters, the opposing pickets began to fraternize. In one instance, a Federal detail and its Confederate opposite struck a humane bargain. The Federals were using a deserted log hut for a post during the day and pulling back closer to camp at night. Confederate cavalry used the same hut by night, withdrawing at first light. The two sides ran into each other one cold morning when the Confederates were slow to leave. Every man reached for a weapon, but no one fired. Instead, they talked. The Confederates asked if the Federals would allow them a few moments to saddle up. That done, they would steal away, and the dual

occupancy of the hut could continue as before. There was agreement all around, and just before the Confederates rode off, someone had another idea: Thereafter, until fighting resumed, each detail would leave a warm fire burning for its foe.

In the Confederate camps, shortages were acute. General Lee spent the early months of 1864 petitioning Richmond for food, for shoes, for warm clothes for his troops. In one dispatch he deplored "the wretched condition of the men, thousands of whom are barefooted, a great number partially shod, and nearly all without overcoats, blankets or warm clothing." Such shortages, Lee advised "are having a bad effect upon the men, both morally and physically."

Richmond, in this third winter of the War, was in poor shape to respond. Commodities were scarce and inflation was rampant in the Confederate capital. Coffee cost $10 a pound, calico $10 a yard. Beans were sold for $60 a bushel, eggs two dollars a dozen. One gold dollar would fetch $30 or more in Confederate paper. Citizens pooled their resources and held "starvation parties" that were marked by a certain desperate gaiety. "There seems to be for the first time," one diarist recorded, "a resolute determination to enjoy the brief hour, and never look beyond the day."

In the field, Confederate soldiers found ways to take their minds off their stomachs. They organized snowball fights that were sometimes fought by entire brigades with colors flying, as if in true battle. And they concocted elaborate practical jokes. Some North Carolina pickets had been watching a house across the Rapidan that appeared to be the headquarters of an enemy officer of considerable rank. The North Carolinians set

Night Assault at the Rappahannock River

To cover the withdrawal after his failed flanking maneuver against General Meade in the autumn of 1863, Robert E. Lee set up a mile-long bridgehead on the north bank of the Rappahannock River near Rappahannock Station. On November 7, Lee went to bed believing the position secure in the hands of General Harry Hays and 2,300 of his Louisiana Tigers, plus three regiments of North Carolinians. But then disaster struck.

Spearheaded by the 6th Maine and the 5th Wisconsin, soldiers of Federal VI Corps came out of the blackness, cheering as they charged the earthworks. Savage hand-to-hand fighting broke out; soldiers clubbed, stabbed and fired at close range along the line. Sergeant Otis Roberts of the 6th Maine entered the fray well in advance of his unit and was immediately surrounded by Confederates, who forced him to surrender. A moment later, when Roberts' comrades caught up and stormed the position, the young sergeant cried, "I take it back!" and snatched the colors of the 8th Louisiana.

The battle surged back and forth until a second charge led by youthful Colonel Emory Upton gave the Union regiments a decisive edge. Broken, the Confederates fled across a bridge or tried to swim to the south bank of the river, having lost four cannon, eight battleflags and 1,303 men. In the South, the Battle of Rappahannock Station was called a "mortifying disaster." The Union celebrated a victory that marked the first successful night attack of the War.

Major General Harry Thompson Hays, who commanded the unsuccessful defense of the bridgehead at Rappahannock Station, narrowly avoided capture. Although Hays was surrounded by Federals, his horse bolted and the general escaped, galloping to safety through hostile fire.

Brigadier General David Russell was so sure of his troops' "well known character" that he proposed the risky night attack and then led the assault on the Confederate bridgehead. Russell was wounded. He recovered in time to command his men in the Wilderness but was later killed in the Third Battle of Winchester.

Stabbed by a bayonet, a Confederate color-bearer falls before the charging Federals in the moonlit action at the Battle of Rappahannock Station.

about making a so-called Quaker cannon. They found wagon wheels with a tongue attached, mounted a huge hollow log on it and provided themselves with a rammer and some large stones.

At a signal, the Carolinians dashed with their creation almost to the river, wheeled it into position and pointed it at the house opposite. With loud words of command they rammed a stone into the log and seemed about to demolish the Federal headquarters. "For a time there was considerable commotion on the other side," wrote a young Confederate staff officer, Lieutenant McHenry Howard. "The picket line hurriedly prepared for action and the house was speedily emptied, the inmates not standing in any order in going, but making for the woods at once. Presently the joke was appreciated and, with much laughter, the lines resumed their status."

There came a day, late in winter, when the games of war turned real—at least for one dramatic flurry. Brigadier General Judson Kilpatrick, a swashbuckling, ambitious 28-year-old cavalry division commander had managed to get President Lincoln's ear with a scheme to raid Richmond. Kilpatrick's purpose was to liberate the nearly 15,000 Federal prisoners incarcerated there. Lincoln admired the plan's boldness. He also had recently issued a proclamation offering amnesty to any Confederate citizen who would pledge allegiance to the Union, and Kilpatrick promised to distribute thousands of copies of the President's offer as he rode through enemy country.

General Meade was issued orders from Washington to cover Kilpatrick with a diversion. On February 28, grumbling but obedi-

ent, Meade sent Major General John Sedgwick's VI Corps marching ostentatiously to the Federal right, in the direction of Gordonsville. Brigadier General George Custer's cavalry brigade also spurred off to the west. Lee's army looked to its left. That night, Kilpatrick's 3,500 troopers crossed the Rapidan on the Confederate right at Ely's Ford, scattered the pickets they encountered and set out under a clear, starry sky for Richmond. They moved with six field pieces and five days' rations, intending to strike and be back behind Union lines before the Confederates knew what had hit them.

At the crossroads settlement of Spotsylvania Court House, Kilpatrick split his force. He sent 500 men riding west under Colonel Ulric Dahlgren. Dahlgren was the dashing son of Rear Admiral John Dahlgren, inventor of the bottle-shaped Dahlgren gun

General William French, whose facial twitch won him the sobriquet "Old Blinkey," bore much of the blame for the Union failure at Mine Run. A drinking problem may have contributed to his sluggishness during the campaign; one of his men related that at dawn on the first day of the battle the General was already "fuller'n a goat."

Generals George Meade and William French confer during the Union advance at Mine Run. Later, after Meade detached two of French's divisions and assigned them to General Gouverneur Warren — who then refused to attack — French angrily confronted Meade. "You've taken all my troops away from me and have given them to a beardless boy and for what?" shouted French. "Why don't we hear the sounds of his guns?"

much admired by the U.S. Navy. At 21, Ulric Dahlgren was one of the youngest colonels in the Federal Army. He was in the saddle despite an artificial leg, the result of a wound suffered just after Gettysburg. His mission now was to circle southward, cross the James River and penetrate Richmond from the south, freeing prisoners and scattering the amnesty proclamations. At the same time, Kilpatrick and the main body of troopers would approach the city from the north and draw the brunt of Richmond's defense. The city was known to be well fortified, but its earthworks were accurately believed to be manned mostly by militia.

Kilpatrick's force rode all night and the next day. The weather deteriorated and the sky rained ice, chilling the cavalry's fervor. With night came absolute darkness; the sleet fell harder and low branches stiffened by ice

tormented the troopers. They rode down blind paths, running into trees or one another. Some of the horses went down, not to rise again, and the men began to understand why their commander's nickname was "Kill Cavalry."

By midmorning on March 1, Kilpatrick had reined up five miles outside Richmond, deployed a skirmish line and positioned his field guns. The troopers could see Richmond's fortifications, but there was no sign of Dahlgren, who was supposed to be in the city by now. Kilpatrick touched off his guns, expecting to hear an answering volley from Dahlgren. Instead, he drew brisk fire from Confederate cannon. The defenders of Richmond had been alerted, and 500 men with six guns blocked any approach from the north while the city's Local Defense Brigade guarded the south and west.

35

Through the cold day, Kilpatrick's worn-out cavalry sparred with the Confederates at long range. At dark, with still no sign of Dahlgren, Kilpatrick wheeled his troopers back a few miles and went into bivouac. No one had slept for two days, but few of the men were able to sleep this night either. "A more dreary, dismal night it would be difficult to imagine," one cavalryman remembered, "with rain, snow, sleet, mud, cold and wet to the skin, rain and snow falling rapidly, the roads a puddle of mud and the night as dark as pitch."

Before the night was over, an attack by Confederate cavalry added to the Federals' discomfort. No militia these, but some of Lee's finest. Commanded by Major General Wade Hampton, the Confederates had been pursuing the Union band ever since it had crossed the Rapidan. Hampton had brought with him two field pieces, and their fire sparked the inky night, slinging case shot into the Federals at close range. Kilpatrick's men managed to withstand the attack, but they were forced to fall back even farther from Richmond, sniped at by Hampton's troopers, before they could rest. Late the next day, the mystery of Dahlgren's whereabouts was partially solved when about 300 of Dahlgren's riders straggled into Kilpatrick's camp. They told an unhappy tale.

Riding west, Dahlgren's party had picked up a black youth named Martin Robinson, who said he could lead the raiders to a ford on the James River. But when the Federals reached the chosen place, they found the river too swollen to cross. Young Dahlgren, in a burst of anger, ordered the guide hanged on the spot. Unable to cross, the troopers continued eastward down the James on the wrong side, now far behind schedule. By March 1, despite prickly resistance by the Local Defense Brigade, they had pressed to within three miles of the city. But any hope of surprise had vanished and Kilpatrick had pulled back by then. Dahlgren, too, gave up the venture and ordered a withdrawal. It was a desperate ride, through driving sleet, with unseen Confederates sniping from behind every barn and bush. In the dark, the Federal column broke in two. One half found its way to Kilpatrick.

Dahlgren, at the head of perhaps 200 men, was not so fortunate. He made a dash for the northeast and crossed the Mattaponi River, only to run into an ambush set up by a mixed force of Confederate cavalry and local militia. Revolver in hand, Dahlgren challenged the encircling enemy: "Surrender, you damned Rebels, or I'll shoot you!" Four bullets from the responding volley took the Federal's life. In the next few minutes, all but a few of his men were run down—some killed, but most captured.

Kilpatrick and his survivors managed to scramble back to the Union lines. But the Richmond raid had failed, at a cost of 340 Federal casualties as well as 1,000 horses killed, captured or rendered unfit for service. Like discarded newspapers, Lincoln's amnesty proclamations blew unheeded across the land. There would be no more fighting in Virginia until a new general took command; and Grant was on his way.

Spring was budding through Virginia in late March when Lieutenant General Grant commandeered a plain brick house in Culpeper and had tents pitched on the lawn for his staff. He was just down the road from General Meade's headquarters at Brandy Station and—as Northern newspapers

General George Armstrong Custer *(mounted, with braided sleeve)* questions Confederate prisoners during a foray into Albemarle County, Virginia, in late February 1864 that was meant to divert attention from the Kilpatrick-Dahlgren raid. The scene was sketched by the prolific artist Alfred Waud, who took the opportunity to record himself for posterity *(mounted right of center, with beard).*

were quick to point out — six miles closer to the front.

Having settled into his new post, Grant, on March 29, reviewed the proud veterans of V Corps. For many of the men this was their first look at the new commander, and most of them were unimpressed. "Just as General Grant came on the ground it commenced to rain," Artillery Colonel Charles Wainwright recorded in his diary. "He rode along the line in a slouchy unobservant way, with his coat unbuttoned and setting anything but an example of military bearing to the troops. There was no enthusiasm, and as the rain increased, we were quickly dismissed without passing in review."

Grant's reputation had preceded him. In Northern households his initials were said to stand for "Unconditional Surrender." Yet a

vein of skepticism ran through the Army of the Potomac. As Grant heard until he was sick of it, "You've never met Bobby Lee and his boys, and mind you, Lee is just over the Rapidan."

And one of Grant's opening moves was not popular. To streamline the army, Grant disbanded the understrength I and III Corps — which had been decimated at Gettysburg — and distributed the men between II and V Corps. The abolition of those proud commands did not endear the new commander to the battle-hardened veterans. But if they were disgruntled, the soldiers were at least disposed to give their taciturn new general a chance. "He cannot be weaker or more inefficient than the generals who have wasted the lives of our comrades during the past three years," wrote one soldier in his diary.

Grant made remarkably few changes at the top of the army's command. He did select a new leader for its Cavalry Corps: Philip H. Sheridan, a cocky and aggressive 33-year-old major general who had distinguished himself at Stones River and in the storming of Missionary Ridge. Almost all of Sheridan's experience had been with infantry, and he certainly did not look the part of a cavalry commander. Bandy-legged and wiry, he stood but five feet six inches tall; hard months in the field had reduced him to a shadow at 115 pounds. When Sheridan arrived in Washington on April 4, Halleck introduced him around at the War Department and a headquarters man later remarked snidely to Grant, "That officer you brought on from the West is rather a little fellow to handle your cavalry." But Grant, who had seen Sheridan in action at Chattanooga, replied, "You will find him big enough for the purpose before we get through with him."

Grant was counting on using his Cavalry Corps as a concentrated striking force. Even more clearly, he saw that numbers could be the key to a Union victory. Through Halleck, Grant instructed the Union's farflung departmental commanders to pare their garrisons and dispatch the extra men to Virginia. Closer to home, he evicted thousands of troops from their comfortable postings within the elaborate fortifications of Washington. Most of these so-called paper-collar soldiers were Heavy Artillerymen — drilled in the use of the big guns but also able to function as infantry. They had had an easy war so far, spending each night in a barracks bed with a full belly. Such assignments were coveted, and the duty roster of the Heavy Artillery regiments had become outlandishly swollen. Now many of these regiments were

marched through the mud to the camp on the Rapidan, where the veterans greeted the newcomers with derision.

Grant also set about converting Washington's excess cavalrymen into infantry. Many of these troopers had been languishing in the capital, waiting for remounts — but not all. One colonel who rode into Washington that spring at the head of 1,200 handsomely mounted Pennsylvanians was abruptly relieved of his horses. His men were furnished with muskets and were soon on their way to the Rapidan, on foot. Grant also reduced the number of headquarters wagons. From now on there would be only one per regiment, one per brigade and perhaps two for a division headquarters. This move threw scores of teamsters and muleskinners into the ranks. "You needn't laugh at me," a driver was heard shouting at a braying mule one day. "You may be in the ranks yourself before Grant gets through with the Army."

Another change, aimed at sustaining the North's numerical superiority, was initiated by Secretary of War Stanton and approved by Grant. For three years, the Union and the Confederacy had routinely exchanged prisoners. Now the Union put a stop to the practice; the North could replace such losses from its larger population but the South could not. The move provided Grant's soldiers with a fresh incentive to avoid capture. They knew that the Confederacy could barely feed itself, much less its prisoners of war. In the future, capture would mean nothing less than slow starvation.

Despite these measures, the Union faced a potentially disastrous manpower problem in 1864. This was the year of discharges: Those men who had patriotically enlisted for a term of three years after Fort Sumter — and

The Mysterious Legacy of a Slain Colonel

After Colonel Ulric Dahlgren was killed during the abortive cavalry raid on Richmond, the Confederates who shot him discovered papers on his body — or said they did — that sent a tremor through the South. The papers, whose authenticity has never been established, stated that Dahlgren intended to burn the city of Richmond and murder Confederate President Jefferson Davis.

The documents threw Richmond into a furor. Charges of atrocity were leveled at the Union. General Lee called the raid a "barbarous and inhuman plot" and in a formal protest to Meade asked if Dahlgren's intentions reflected the policy of the United States. Meade was quick to respond that the plot, if there was one, had existed only in Dahlgren's mind, but the outraged Confederacy was not mollified. The Richmond *Examiner* savagely mocked the dead colonel, using his supposed words against him: "He has 'swept through the city of Richmond' on a pine bier and 'written his name' on the scrolls of infamy, instead of 'on the hearts of his countrymen.' "

Only Jefferson Davis himself seemed unruffled by the threat. He merely chuckled when he read the words "Davis and Cabinet must be killed on the spot" and then, turning to his secretary of state, placidly remarked, "That means you, Mr. Benjamin."

Colonel Ulric Dahlgren, shown here in a portrait made prior to the skirmish at Hagerstown, where he lost a leg, was unrestrained in his enthusiasm for the planned raid on the Confederate capital. "If successful," he wrote to his father, "it will be the grandest thing on record."

Dahlgren's raiders charge headlong into a devastating Confederate ambush. "Every tree was occupied," wrote cavalryman Louis Beaudrye, one of the Federals

Colonel Dahlgren's bloodstained gauntlet and sash *(above)* were taken from his body along with his wooden leg. Scavengers also cut off one of his fingers in order to get a ring that was stuck. Below are the papers that sparked the Confederate outrage. Although the handwriting is almost certainly Dahlgren's, the colonel's father and numerous other supporters steadfastly maintained that the papers had been forged or altered.

who escaped, "and the bushes poured forth a sheet of fire."

who, as Sherman put it, had been through "the dearest school on earth" — would soon be entitled to go home. Almost half of the North's fighting force was eligible, including many of the crack regiments in the Army of the Potomac.

The Federal government went all out to inspire reenlistments. It offered each man who signed up again a 30-day furlough and $400, to be supplemented by whatever bounty the man's state would come up with. The cash, as one veteran concluded, "seemed to be about the right amount for spending money while on a furlough."

Pride and peer pressure also came into play. A man who chose to reenlist could wear a stripe on his sleeve as evidence that he had been in the fight from the start and was now

Federal cavalry commander Judson Kilpatrick (*fourth from left*) appears confident in this photograph with members of his staff taken just after his raid on Richmond. Kilpatrick's lantern jaw and thick sideburns gave him an odd appearance; one officer remarked that it was hard to look at him without laughing.

serving of his own free will. If at least three quarters of a regiment reenlisted, the regiment — after home leave — would remain intact, retaining its name and its colors. If not, the individuals who reenlisted would be scattered among outfits strange to them. Regimental officers, faced with the possibility of losing their commands, politicked shamelessly among their men.

The temptation to let others take up the cause was strong. "I have no desire to monopolize all the patriotism there is," wrote a veteran from Massachusetts, "but am willing to give others a chance."

In the end, more than half of those eligible for discharge chose to fight on — swayed by the bounty, the prospect of a long furlough and by the stubborn feeling that they should not walk away from a job unfinished. "If they can't kill you in three years, they want you for three more," groused another New Englander. "But I will stay."

Those who reenlisted were joined by fresh volunteers, draftees and hired substitutes. The tent city north of the Rapidan was burgeoning. Infantry, artillery and cavalry drilled relentlessly under Grant's silent gaze, and a grudging respect for the general from the West grew among the men of the Army of the Potomac. "We all felt at last that *the boss* had arrived," declared a soldier from New England, and another youth from Wisconsin wrote home that "Grant wants soldiers, not yaupers."

Grant reciprocated the respect. On April 26 he wrote, "The Army of the Potomac is in splendid condition and evidently feels like whipping somebody. I feel much better with this command than I did before seeing it." The next day Grant turned 42 years old and used the occasion to write to his wife, Julia:

"I am still very well. Don't know exactly the day when I will start, or whether Lee will come here before I am ready to move. Would not tell you if I did know. . . ."

But every veteran knew the change of season would bring a resumption of the carnage. On the day that Grant wrote his wife, Private Robert G. Carter of the 22nd Massachusetts sent a letter to his parents: "The summer days are almost here, when we shall be wearily plodding over the roads once more in search of *victory* or *death*. Many a poor fellow will find the latter. I dread the approaching campaign. I can see horrors insurmountable through the summer months."

Across the river, Lee had been watching his enemy's tent metropolis grow. He had all but despaired of receiving additional provisions: "There is nothing to be had in this section for man or animals," he wrote Jefferson Davis on April 12. What Lee needed most urgently now was men. Longstreet was returning from Tennessee, but a brigade commanded by Brigadier General Robert Hoke had been detached from Lee for service on the coast of North Carolina. And Major General George Pickett's division — the remnants of his charge at Gettysburg — was south of Richmond, containing the Federal coastal garrisons and searching for food. Diplomatically, Lee implored Davis to make his Army of Northern Virginia whole again. "We shall have to glean troops from every quarter," he wrote in mid-April, "to oppose the apparent combination of the enemy."

But an ostensible build-up was not enough to sway Davis, who liked to say that his Administration possessed no "department of anticipation." He would rearrange the Confederacy's troop dispositions only when re-

This rare wartime picture of Robert E. Lee, taken early in 1864, is the only photograph in which the general wears his military sash and dress sword. A Virginia sculptor used the image to create a small statue of Lee, which was sold to benefit disabled Confederate veterans. On the table at left are Lee's sword belt, field glasses, Colt Navy revolver, hat and gauntlets. Below the table are his riding boots. The camp table itself was carved for Lee by his mess boy; the removable top was a checkerboard on the reverse side.

ality compelled him to. Davis' strategy for this fourth year of war was simple: to make the coming offensive so costly for the Union that, by November, the weary and grieving Northern electorate would turn out Lincoln and replace him with a man who would be willing to negotiate peace.

The spring began tragically for Jefferson Davis. On the last day of April, as he was eating lunch at his office desk, a household slave rushed in, bawling that Davis' five-year-old son, Joe, had fallen from a rear balcony to a brick courtyard 30 feet below. The Southern White House was four blocks from the President's office, and when Davis got there he found Joe unconscious. The boy died minutes later. The Davises had three other children, but Joe had been the President's favorite. Davis was inconsolate; when a courier arrived that afternoon with an urgent dispatch from General Lee, the President stared at the message and tried to comprehend it. But he could not focus. "I must have this day with my little son," he said. Davis went upstairs to a bedroom across from the boy's and through that night he paced the floor, intoning: "Not mine, O Lord, but thine."

Lee's latest message was his most urgent appeal yet. "Everything indicates a concentrated attack on this front, which renders me the more anxious to get back the troops belonging to this army, & causes me to suggest if possible, that others be moved from points at the south, where they can be spared, to Richmond." Lee at this hour had only 61,000 men at hand to confront Grant's swelling host of 122,000.

Lee knew from his scouts that time was short. On March 26, the wives of the Federal officers had begun leaving the camp across the river. On April 7, the enemy army had started sending away the sutlers.

On Monday, May 2, Lee mounted Traveller — the seven-year-old "Confederate gray," as Lee called his horse — and with his ranking officers ascended Clark's Mountain, at 700 feet the highest lookout point available. Curving around the foot of the mountain was the Rapidan, brown, flat and 200 feet wide. Across the river lay the Union army. Due east, about 13 miles downstream, was Germanna Ford, and a few miles farther, Ely's Ford. South of the fords sprawled a gray-green expanse called the Wilderness, 12 miles wide and six miles deep. If Grant could get his army swiftly through this nasty tangle of briers, ridges, hillocks, stunted pines and dense undergrowth, he could use his superior numbers to smash Lee in open country.

Grant's alternative would be to move by his right flank, west of where Lee now stood on Clark's Mountain. In doing that, Grant would be following the line of the Orange & Alexandria Railroad, toward Gordonsville, eventually to engage Lee in open country there. A move to the right would give Grant favorable terrain, but it would expose the Union line of communications and in fact uncover Washington itself. A move to the left, fording the Rapidan into the forbidding Wilderness, would keep the moving army always within reach of tidal rivers from which it could be supplied.

Lee studied the terrain through his glasses and understood his opponent's options. Raising a hand encased in a leather gauntlet, he pointed eastward to the two river crossings and told his officers: "Grant will cross by one of those fords."

Sketching the Common Soldier

An easel stands ready in Forbes's tent-studio.

For Edwin Forbes, an artist for Frank Leslie's *Illustrated Newspaper*, being a spectator at the great battles of the Civil War was, in his words, "nearly as dangerous as being a participant." The 22-year-old Forbes attached himself to the Army of the Potomac at the start of the War and stayed on, armed only with a sketchbook, through the siege of Petersburg. Energetic and daring, Forbes edged close to the action in battle after battle. Oblivious of the shells and musket fire, he executed quick sketches that he later refined in hi[s] makeshift tent-studio to the rear.

When the armies were at rest, the ever[-] active Forbes drew the common soldie[r] and camp activity. The Wilderness Cam[-] paign saw Forbes's talents at their peak[.] His sketches, a sampling of which are pre[-] sented on these pages, provide an unglam[-] orized view of the campaign, full of th[e] details that were, as Forbes wrote, "to[o] plain for misunderstanding and far to[o] terrible for any forgetting."

Forbes marveled at the multitude of mule-drawn supply wagons, such as the one shown here, that traveled with the army and "filled the roads on the march."

A teamster known only as Joe leans casually against his wagon. Forbes respected the ability and dedication of the black drivers; he said they seemed to have an "occult understanding" with their mule teams.

Drummer boys, according to Forbes, were "the most picturesque little figures in the Union army." He added that their pranks and high spirits gave "much life to camp or march."

With a pipe in one hand and a newspaper in the other, a weary soldier takes his ease. The men seized such moments whenever they could; Forbes once observed a skirmisher reading while sheltered behind a boulder in the midst of battle.

On February 22, 1864, General Hancock's II Corps holds a ball to celebrate George Washington's birthday. The timber and canvas "ballroom" south of Brandy Station was erected and decorated by the troops for the occasion, and the officers' wives and lady friends were brought in by special train.

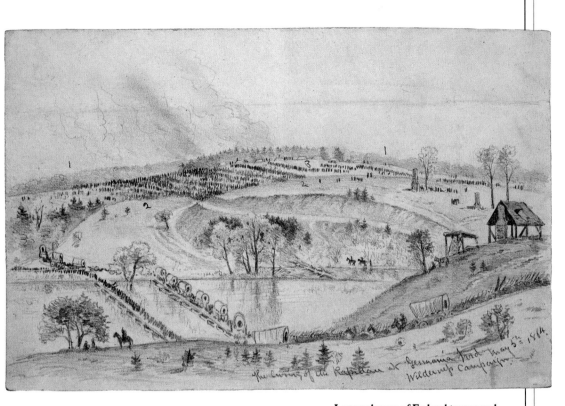

Long columns of Federal troops and wagon trains cross the Rapidan River on pontoon bridges at Germanna Ford on May 5, 1864, heading east toward a fateful meeting with Robert E. Lee's Confederates in the Wilderness. In the background, Union soldiers mass atop a hill and smoke billows from the opening artillery fire.

East of the Rapidan, the Army of the Potomac's line of march in the Wilderness took Federal soldiers past the ruins of the Chancellor house, a grim reminder of their costly defeat one year earlier at the Battle of Chancellorsville.

Men of General Sedgwick's VI Corps
exchange fire with Confederates
deep in the Wilderness, while at their
feet wounded comrades try to crawl
to safety. In the dense thickets of
this battleground, Forbes had to get
dangerously close to the action to
record such scenes.

Lashed on by their drivers, artillery
horses drag a cannon up a muddy incline. The dead horse beside the path
was a victim of an earlier passage.

Soldiers of II Corps lounge behind their log breastworks near the Spotsylvania Court House. Some of the men on the other side of the works are clearing a field of fire in preparation for the coming battle.

May 11th 1864. The Wilderness, on the Brock road

Wounded soldiers crossing the Rappahannock River at
on a flatboat. After the battle of the Wilderness

Downstream from Fredericksburg,
soldiers in a flatboat haul on a rope to
ferry their wounded comrades across
the Rappahannock. A ramp has
been added to help the injured men in
and out of the boat.

This dilapidated old shack with its outsize chimney caught Forbes's eye near the Spotsylvania battlefield. The scattering of soldiers' dog tents nearby suggests the area was a Federal outpost.

Behind the Union lines at Spotsylvania, General Grant and his staff gather at the right *(11)* while reserve batteries *(10)* stand ready to meet an attack. Fighting is under way beyond the gap in the trees *(2)*, and the ridge in the distance *(1)* marks the position of the Confederates.

Soldiers building a breastwork near Cold Harbor have thrust their bayonets into the ground instead of stacking arms according to regulation.

James Ricketts' troops charge Confederate rifle pits at Cold Harbor, netting hundreds of prisoners and two lines of entrenchments.

From the Chickahominy to the James, by Grant, March-June 1864.

Men of the Army of the Potomac press on from Cold Harbor toward the James. In this strung-out procession, a soldier pauses to light his pipe from a brush fire.

Into the Wilderness

"All circumstances seemed to combine to make the scene one of unutterable horror. It was as though Christian men had turned to fiends, and hell itself has usurped the place of earth."

LIEUTENANT COLONEL HORACE PORTER, U.S.A., IN THE WILDERNESS

As the Federal advance began on Wednesday, May 4, Lieutenant Colonel Theodore Lyman, an officer on General George Meade's staff, sat on a bank of the Rapidan River at Germanna Ford and watched the Federal V and VI Corps cross on newly floated pontoon bridges. "How strange it would be," he wondered in his diary, "if each man who was destined to fall in the campaign ahead had some large badge on!" If wonder had been reality, the imposing sight of a great army on the move would have assumed a funereal aspect: Almost half of the men Lyman saw would have been so marked. Eleven terrible days after the first blueclad troops stepped out, Lyman would wearily note in his diary that he felt as though six months had passed.

On that first day Major Abner R. Small of the 16th Maine recalled marching through the early-morning darkness into "a glorious spring day. Wildflowers were up; I remember them nodding by the roadside. Everything was bright and blowing." Spring had sounded the bell, and the two armies, like two scarred old pugilists, closed on each other for one more punishing round.

V Corps, under General Gouverneur Warren, crossed first at Germanna Ford. Warren was a 34-year-old former chief engineer of the Army of the Potomac. An ill-tempered commander, he was admired by his men, detested by his officers and not always quick to obey a superior's order. He had distinguished himself the previous July at Little Round Top; in December his reliability had been questioned when he ignored Meade's instructions to attack the formidable Confederate position at Mine Run.

Next across the Rapidan was VI Corps, Major General John Sedgwick in command. Sedgwick, who liked playing solitaire in his tent, also enjoyed the affection of his men, who called him "Uncle John." A writer of the day lauded him as "the exemplar of the steadfast soldierly obedience to duty: Singularly gentle and childlike in character, he was scarcely more beloved in his own command than throughout the army." Grant considered him an officer who "was never at fault when serious work was to be done." Sedgwick was 50 years old. If Lyman, the diarist, had realized his fantasy, Sedgwick would have been one of those wearing a large badge.

II Corps, now led by Major General Winfield Scott Hancock, crossed at Ely's Ford, six miles east of Germanna. Hancock "the Superb," as he was called, was back in action but still suffering from a near-fatal wound he had received at Gettysburg. "The beau ideal of a soldier," wrote an admiring correspondent, "blue-eyed, fair haired Saxon, strong, well proportioned and manly, broad chested, full and compact." At 40, Hancock had a reputation for aggressiveness in combat that matched his knightly looks. His II Corps would suffer more casualties — and capture more prisoners — in the days ahead than the rest of the Army of the Potomac combined.

Still another force was available to the

This slouch hat, pierced by a bullet at the rear left edge of the crown, bears the clover-leaf emblem of the Federal II Corps. Its owner, Captain Charles Nash of the 19th Maine, was leading a company against General James Longstreet's Confederates in the Wilderness on May 6, 1864, when a bullet sent the hat flying; Nash was not harmed.

Union offensive. This was IX Corps, held back for the moment to protect the rebuilt Orange & Alexandria Railroad from Manassas Junction south to Rappahannock Station. In command was Major General Ambrose E. Burnside, aged 39. Burnside's reputation, tarnished by his defeat at Fredericksburg in 1862, had been partially restored, in Grant's view, by his successful defense of Knoxville the previous fall. Since he outranked Meade, Burnside had an independent corps and he reported directly to Grant. Burnside would not distinguish himself in the hard days to come.

The Federal tactics, as defined by Meade's chief of staff, Brigadier General Andrew A. Humphreys, depended on a quick start: "By setting the whole army in motion at midnight, it might move so far beyond the Rapidan the first day that it would be able to pass out of the Wilderness and turn, or partially turn, the right flank of Lee before a general engagement took place."

Robert E. Lee was soon aware of the Federal advance and was determined to meet it. By 9 a.m. on May 4, scouting reports had confirmed Lee's prediction of a crossing on the Confederate right. The general realized the import of the looming battle. The night before, in his headquarters at Orange Court House, about 20 miles southwest of the Wilderness, Lee had written stoically: "If victorious, we have everything to live for. If defeated, there will be nothing left to live for."

Lee's main force was outnumbered nearly 2 to 1 but had the advantage of operating on interior lines and in familiar territory. Lee's army had three corps, each under a commander who had seen much — almost too much — of the War. Closest to the advancing Federals was Lieutenant General Richard S. Ewell's II Corps, in the vicinity of Mine Run. Ewell's troops called him "Old Baldhead." At Groveton in 1862 a Minié ball had smashed the bones in one of his knees and the leg had to be sawed away. The loss made riding a challenge. An attendant had to help the 47-year-old Ewell into the saddle of his horse, an unimpressive gray named Rifle.

Upstream on the Rapidan, south of Ewell, was A. P. Hill's III Corps. Hill, aged 38, had served with distinction as a division commander under Stonewall Jackson, who had been mortally wounded at nearby Chancellorsville almost exactly a year before. Hill had inherited Jackson's corps, but after 11 months in command he still lacked confidence in himself. And he had become worn and pale after suffering for months from some undiagnosed ailment. His health was about to fail him.

Ten miles south of Hill, seeking good forage around Gordonsville, was Confederate I Corps under Lieutenant General James Longstreet, newly returned from the campaign in Tennessee. Lee's "Old Warhorse" was still smarting over the failure of the campaign at Knoxville and he was more eager

than ever to prove himself. On May 4, he and his corps were at an uncomfortable distance — more than 30 miles' march — from the Wilderness.

Lee's cavalry, as always, was in the hands of the flamboyant Jeb Stuart. Now barely past 30, Stuart's brilliant star had been sullied during the Gettysburg Campaign. He had done well since then, but his cavalry was being worn down by a chronic shortage of horses and fodder. Stuart had more than 8,000 troopers in three divisions to match Philip Sheridan's 12,000. Around the first of May, Stuart's troopers were strung out well to the east, as far away as Fredericksburg, scouting the Rapidan while searching for spring forage for their hungry horses.

Three roads, roughly parallel, led eastward from Lee's infantry encampments in-

to the Wilderness. They were the Orange Turnpike, which ran from Orange Court House through Chancellorsville and continued to Fredericksburg; the Orange Plank road, about two miles south of the Turnpike; and the Catharpin road, another two or three miles farther south. All three intersected with the route that the southbound Federals would eventually have to defend, the Brock road. On receiving word that his enemy was moving, Lee ordered Ewell forward along the Turnpike. He then instructed A. P. Hill to send two divisions forward on the Orange Plank road, while leaving Major General Richard H. Anderson's division to guard against any surprise attack across the upper fords of the Rapidan. Longstreet, farther away than the others, would move up along the Catharpin road.

Trailed by a long train of supply wagons, troops of John Sedgwick's VI Corps cross a pontoon bridge over the Rapidan River at Germanna Ford on the afternoon of May 4. Before them, wrote a Federal soldier, lay the Wilderness, "reaching back in mysterious silence."

Lee chose to ride with Hill. The commander mounted Traveller and waited for Hill's men to strike their tents. They were quick about it. "We received orders to cook rations immediately and prepare for the march," Captain James F. J. Caldwell of the 1st South Carolina recalled. "We at once set to work, but before half the bread could be baked the command was given to fall in. Knapsacks were packed, blankets rolled up, half-cooked dough or raw meal thrust into haversacks, the accumulated plunder of nine months thrown into the streets, accoutrements girded on, arms taken, and in half an hour we were on the march."

U. S. Grant crossed the Rapidan around noon, riding Cincinnati, his big bay. Grant had donned sword, belt and sash for the oc-

casion, along with frock coat and a general's gold cord around his black slouch hat. In his pockets were two dozen cigars, a day's supply. He was accompanied by a civilian friend, Congressman Elihu B. Washburne of Illinois. It was Washburne, from Grant's home district in Galena, who had sponsored the bill creating the rank of lieutenant general that Grant now held. The marching soldiers speculated aloud about who this stranger in the black coat might be. One suggested glumly that Grant had brought along his own undertaker.

On the south bank of the Rapidan, Grant established temporary headquarters at a deserted farmhouse, and from its dilapidated front steps he watched Sedgwick's corps follow Warren's across Germanna Ford. His reverie was interrupted by a newspaper correspondent who stepped up to ask, "General Grant, about how long will it take you to get to Richmond?" It was a question without an answer, but Grant, his wry side showing, responded at once. "I will agree to be there in about four days," he said. "That is, if General Lee becomes party to the agreement; but if he objects, the trip will undoubtedly be prolonged."

Word soon came that Federal signal officers had deciphered a Confederate message sent to General Ewell: "We are moving." Clearly Lee was advancing to intercept the Federals. With that information, Grant sent off a dispatch to Burnside, in the rear: Abandon the railroad and bring the reserve IX Corps forward to the river crossing, marching all night if necessary.

Early in the afternoon, the Army of the Potomac halted in the Wilderness. The men could have kept going, but their vast wagon train was already lagging behind, and it had to be protected. Grant's military secretary, Lieutenant Colonel Adam Badeau, remarked that if a battle were fought in these thickets, it would be "a wrestle as blind as midnight." Others knew from experience how cruel the place could be, for they had been in the thick of the Battle of Chancellorsville here one year ago.

Hancock's II Corps, having crossed at Ely's Ford, bivouacked at the Chancellorsville crossroads near the ruin of the old Chancellor house, which had burned during the fighting in 1863. There were skeletons here, uncovered by the rains of winter. An infantryman kicked at a skull and told his comrades: "This is what you are all coming to, and some of you will start toward it tomorrow."

Five miles to the west, at the intersection of Warren's route and the Orange Turnpike, V Corps's troops made camp around an abandoned stage station called Wilderness Tavern; Sedgwick's corps extended back to Germanna Ford, to cover the endless passage of the wagons. The men did not sing, as they had in winter camp. There was little talk. One New York soldier remembered "a sense of ominous dread, which many of us found it almost impossible to shake off."

When Lee's columns halted for the night, the two sides were only five miles apart; but neither realized how close it was to the other's main force. Ewell, moving down the Turnpike, had penetrated two or three miles into the Wilderness; his lead elements stopped at a place called Locust Grove. Lee, with Hill's two divisions, camped five miles southwest of Ewell around a settlement on the Orange Plank road called New Verdiersville (the men dubbed it "My Dearsville"). Lee assumed that Grant would either turn west, toward Mine Run, or turn east and march on Fredericksburg. Before going to bed, Lee sent his adjutant, Colonel Walter Taylor, to instruct Ewell to resume his march down the pike early the next day and engage whatever side of the enemy he encountered. Despite cautions from Lee to limit his opening attack, Ewell was pleased. "Just the orders I like," he said. "Go straight down the road and strike the enemy wherever I find him."

At a campfire fueled by fence rails near the Rapidan, General Grant sat up till midnight, smoking a cigar and sharing information with George Meade. Telegrams had arrived from Washington reporting that William T. Sherman had advanced in Georgia, Benjamin Butler had begun his ascent of the James River and Franz Sigel's forces were moving

Seated on a log near Germanna Ford on May 4, General Ulysses S. Grant writes a message to Washington as members of his staff stand by. "The crossing of the Rapidan effected," Grant's note read in part. "Forty-eight hours now will demonstrate whether the enemy intends giving battle this side of Richmond."

up the Shenandoah Valley. Grant's strategy of massive concerted attacks was unfolding according to plan.

Eager to get out of the Wilderness, Grant had the Federal army on the move at 5 a.m. on May 5. Lieutenant Colonel Horace Porter of Grant's staff wrote that he expected "either a fight or a foot-race" before nightfall. Hancock launched his II Corps southward from Chancellorsville on a route that crossed the Brock road at Todd's Tavern below the Orange Plank road. Warren, at Wilderness Tavern, deployed one of his divisions down the Orange Turnpike to the west, to shield his flank, and headed south. "I feel lighthearted and confident," he wrote his wife

early that morning. "We are going to have a magnificent campaign."

Warren's troops were soon strung out for three miles along a country lane; the roadway was no more than 20 feet wide in places and hemmed in on both sides by heavy forest. This blind path would intersect with the Orange Plank road at Parker's Store.

Shortly after 7 a.m. the head of Warren's column was at the Chewning farm, a mile shy of Parker's Store, and Hancock's lead elements had already passed Todd's Tavern when orders came from General Meade to halt the movement south. Federal skirmishers had encountered Confederate infantry — Ewell's men — approaching along the Orange Turnpike. The division left behind by Warren to guard the Turnpike, commanded by Brigadier General Charles Griffin, quickly threw up breastworks and sent skirmishers forward to determine, if they could, the enemy's size and intentions.

Meade wanted immediate action. He ordered Warren to attack at once with his entire force. North of the Turnpike, Sedgwick's VI Corps was to advance on Warren's right in support. Grant too wanted action. Once he had seen for himself that Burnside's IX Corps, after its all-night march, had reached the Rapidan and started to cross at Germanna Ford, Grant rode forward to join Meade near Wilderness Tavern. Meade at first thought the Confederate advance was no more than a delaying action. "I think Lee is making a demonstration to gain time," he wrote in a message to Grant. "I shall, if such is the case, punish him."

But the urge proved quicker than the deed, and hours of halting maneuver would pass before the "blind wrestle" could begin in earnest. Sedgwick, moving down the Germanna Plank road, sent a division commanded by Brigadier General Horatio G. Wright westward through the briers in the hope that he would link with Griffin's right flank. But the only route available to Wright was a path — the so-called Culpeper Mine road — that was overgrown and nearly impassable. Until Wright arrived, V Corps's right flank was unprotected.

Warren's lead divisions, spread out along the track to Parker's Store, formed their lines. Facing northwest — with little room to maneuver — they prepared to advance into the trackless, clutching undergrowth.

The division closest to Griffin was commanded by Brigadier General James Wads-

worth, a genial, white-haired Harvard man of 56 who had once studied law under Daniel Webster. It now fell to Wadsworth to lead his men through the choking thickets to find Griffin's bare left flank. Wadsworth had led troops from Bull Run to Gettysburg, but never in country like this. Which way? he asked Warren. The corps commander consulted his pocket compass and told Wadsworth to march his division due west. The troops plunged into the undergrowth and at length, with great difficulty and no small amount of luck, managed to link up with Griffin's threatened line.

Farther south, meanwhile, along the Orange Plank road, a detachment of Federal cavalry had run into A. P. Hill's advance guard near Parker's Store. Using their Spencer carbines to good effect, the Federal troopers fired and slowly fell back.

General Lee, who was riding with Hill, was aware that his army was not prepared for a major action. Longstreet's corps, though moving, was still a day's march away. Cautiously, Lee sent word to Ewell on the Turnpike around 8 a.m. to moderate his advance to match Hill's slow progress up the Orange Plank road.

By now Ewell had seen enough signs of the enemy to know that he was in for a fight, and he began forming his men for action. To his front, astride the Turnpike, was a large, bramble-covered clearing known as Sanders' Field. On the east edge of the field Ewell deployed the four brigades of General Edward Johnson's division and extended the line farther south with the troops of Major General Robert E. Rodes's division.

No sooner had Ewell issued orders to "fall back slowly, if pressed," than Griffin's Federal battle line came swarming out of the foliage. The hour was past noon. North of the Turnpike, Brigadier General Romeyn Ayres's brigade attacked, led by the 140th New York Zouaves and elements of five Regular Army regiments. The Federals started across Sanders' Field, pushing through matted brambles and tangled brush; they charged across a gully and ran head on into a curtain of fire from three Confederate brigades in the woods at the east edge of the field. The 140th New York veered left, and the Regulars stopped dead and gave way.

Behind them, Ayres's second line, three Zouave regiments from New York and Pennsylvania, now encountered the hurricane of fire. They passed through the retreating Regulars only to be driven back themselves as volley after volley crashed into their shaken ranks. Most of the attacking regiments fell back to the shelter of the woods, but the 140th and 146th New Yorkers stayed put and renewed the attack.

The 140th charged first, with a shout that its adjutant said "drowned all other sounds."

The skeleton of a soldier lies in the Wilderness near the Orange Plank road. Such stark remains, left after the Battle of Chancellorsville in 1863, greeted the troops as they arrived to do battle in 1864. "We wandered to and fro," one Federal recalled, "looking at the gleaming skulls and whitish bones, and examining the exposed clothing of the dead to see if they had been Union or Confederate soldiers."

The 146th pressed close behind. Now Griffin sent Lieutenant W. H. Shelton with two 12-pounder Napoleons of Battery B, 1st New York Artillery, galloping down the pike to support the Zouaves.

When the New Yorkers neared the trees on the far side of Sanders' Field, they were met by a withering volley at close range. Moments later they were raked by fire from the right flank as well — a Confederate brigade had pushed to the north border of the field. "It seemed as if the regiment had been annihilated," a Zouave recalled.

Lieutenant Shelton had barely unlimbered his two Napoleons on the Turnpike when his artillerymen were hit and began to fall. Under pressure, he loaded and fired his guns — unfortunately into the backs of the Zouaves fighting in the woods to his front. "The shot went plowing through our ranks," wrote Lieutenant Henry Cribben of the 140th New York, "badly demoralizing the heroes who were stemming the tidal wave of bullets pouring in upon them."

Staggered, the New Yorkers nevertheless pushed on into the woods. "Closing with the enemy, we fought them with bayonet as well as bullet," wrote Captain H.W.S. Sweet of the 146th. "Up through the trees rolled dense clouds of battle smoke, circling about the green of the pines and mingling with the white of the flowering dogwoods. Underneath, men ran to and fro, firing, shouting, stabbing with bayonets, beating each other with the butts of their guns. Each man fought on his own resources, grimly and desperately."

Already the Battle of the Wilderness had taken on the nightmarish quality that would define it throughout. Soon the woods were on fire and the flames spread to the dry,

bramble-choked field. The screams of wounded men, hurt too badly to flee, rose above the sounds of battle. By now most of the officers of the two New York regiments had been put out of action and their disorganized men were bolting back across Sanders' Field, pursued by the 1st and 3rd North Carolina of Brigadier General George H. Steuart's brigade. A survivor of the 146th

Three officers of the 4th Georgia — from left to right, Captain Howard Tinsley, Major William Willis and First Lieutenant Eugene Hawkins — sat for this portrait in 1863. As their regiment counterattacked along the Orange Turnpike on May 5, young Hawkins was killed.

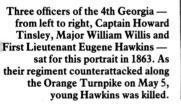

ɛrmer officer of the Tactics Deɪtment at West Point, Brigadier ɪeral John Marshall Jones was ral- ɪg the troops of his Confederate ɪade during the initial fighting ɪg the Orange Turnpike when he ɪ hit and mortally wounded. Gen- ɪ Ewell termed the loss of Jones ɪrreparable one to his brigade.''

recalled vividly that "the bright red of our Zouave uniforms mingled with the sober gray and butternut of the Confederates, creating a fantastic spectacle as the wearers ran over the field, firing and shouting." Together, the 140th and 146th New York lost 567 of their 1,600 men that afternoon.

Shelton's artillerymen fared no better. Most of the battery's horses were shot down, and the gun crews found it impossible to extricate the two Napoleons. The two pieces were destined to sit in no man's land, between the two lines, for the rest of the battle.

Across the Turnpike, meanwhile, one of Griffin's brigades, under Brigadier General Joseph J. Bartlett, pressed the attack across the south part of Sanders' Field, with the famed Iron Brigade of Wadsworth's division hard on the left. The Federals crossed the clearing and slammed into a Virginia brigade under Brigadier General John Marshall Jones. In the brief, violent struggle, the Confederate line splintered and then broke. Jones was killed trying to rally his men, and his aide, Captain Robert D. Early, a nephew of General Jubal Early, fell dead beside him.

A large hole had been opened in Ewell's line, and the Iron Brigade, led by Brigadier General Lysander Cutler, drove through it, pushing the Confederates back. But Wadsworth's Federals to the left of the Iron Brigade were now in trouble. There, one brigade had become mired in the marshy footing next to a stream, disorienting another, under Colonel James C. Rice, on its left. Rice, confused in the thick brush, inadvertently wheeled his left flank across the front of an enemy brigade — North Carolinians under Brigadier General Junius Daniel — that had stood its ground.

At that critical moment, help arrived for the Confederates. Ewell, seeing his center collapsing, had turned his horse and pounded down the Turnpike toward Early's reserve division. On the way, he happened to spot Brigadier General John B. Gordon at the head of his Georgia troops. The corps commander reined in his horse and shouted to Gordon: "Form at once on the right of the turnpike." Gordon's men rushed forward and moved into line beside Daniel's North Carolinians. Together, they opened up on the confused and stationary Federal brigades. Startled by the unexpected volume of fire, Wadsworth's troops staggered and gave way. Their withdrawal spelled an end to the Federal breakthrough — without support on its flank, the Iron Brigade was forced to retreat in turn.

Griffin's attack was over. He had been promised support on his right flank, but what had happened to it? In fact, Horatio Wright's division was still inching through the undergrowth, its march bedeviled by skirmishers from the 1st North Carolina Cavalry and by sharpshooters from the Stonewall Brigade. Without Wright's help, Griffin had only a mounting casualty list to

WOUNDED ZOUAVE OF THE 155TH PENNSYLVANIA

The Peacock Garb of the Zouave Brigade

Among the first Federal units engaged in the Wilderness was Brigadier General Romeyn Ayres's hard-fighting Zouave brigade. Half of Ayres's command was made up of Regular Army battalions, the other half of four volunteer regiments from New York and Pennsylvania. The volunteers had recently been issued colorful uniforms modeled on the garb worn by elite French North African troops. Some examples of these uniforms have been preserved and are shown at right.

The outfits boosted the men's morale. "We had the vanity to think there was no organization in the army superior to us," one officer recalled. But they paid a high price for their enthusiasm in the Wilderness. In little more than half an hour Ayres's brigade suffered 936 casualties, 633 of them Zouaves.

UNIFORM OF
SERGEANT CHAUNCEY SMITH,
146TH NEW YORK

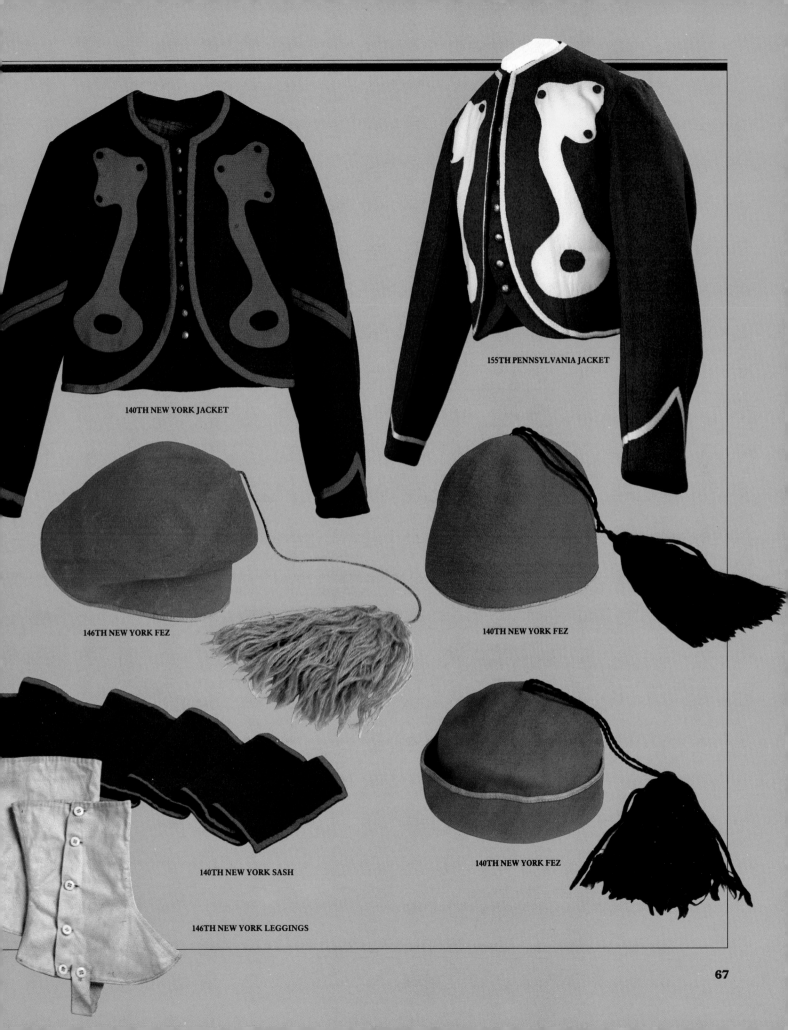

140TH NEW YORK JACKET

155TH PENNSYLVANIA JACKET

146TH NEW YORK FEZ

140TH NEW YORK FEZ

140TH NEW YORK SASH

140TH NEW YORK FEZ

146TH NEW YORK LEGGINGS

show for his efforts. Griffin set his division to building breastworks and spurred his horse toward headquarters, a furious man.

An explosive confrontation ensued. Grant and Meade had established their command post in a clearing just west of where the Germanna Plank road crossed the Orange Turnpike, a mile or more behind the fighting. Grant, his orders given, had found a seat on a tree stump; he unbuttoned his coat as the day grew warmer and began whittling to fill the time as he awaited developments.

Griffin, a bellicose West Pointer, Indian fighter and frustrated three-year veteran of the War, had lost his temper. He leaped off his horse and, ignoring Grant, made straight for Meade, cursing. Warren had let him down, Sedgwick had let him down, the Army had failed him. Meade, whose temper was as hot as any man's, calmly listened and said nothing as Griffin stamped out.

Grant got up and approached Meade. This loud act of insubordination had bothered him. "Who is this General Gregg?" Grant asked, getting the name wrong. "You ought to put him under arrest."

"His name is Griffin, not Gregg," Meade said quietly. "And that's only his way of talking." Then, in an almost fatherly gesture, Meade reached out and buttoned the coat of his younger superior. The tension broke and Grant went back to his whittling.

Both Ewell's and Warren's corps had dug in as best they could, separated by about 300 yards of woodland where flash fires erupted from time to time. The firing continued between half-hidden lines of infantry, but it was a few miles to the south, along the Orange Plank road, that the full weight of the battle was developing.

When General Meade learned at mid-morning that Confederates were advancing in force on the Orange Plank road, he realized that the Federal army was in danger of being sliced in two. If A. P. Hill's two gray-clad divisions could take and hold the junction of the Orange Plank road and the Brock road — the Federals' only accessible north-south route — then Hancock and his II Corps would be cut off from the rest of the Army of the Potomac. Meade sent orders to Hancock, waiting at Todd's Tavern, to countermarch northward to the vital junction. Then Meade dispatched most of a division from Sedgwick's corps — 6,000 well-tested veterans commanded by Brigadier General Richard Getty — south on the Brock road to hold the intersection until Hancock could get there.

Getty, a competent West Pointer, reached the crossing around 11:30 a.m., just as Hill's infantry was dispersing the last of the Federal cavalry that had impeded them all morning. He deployed his men on both sides of the Orange Plank road and sent them forward. When they got to within 50 yards of the Confederates, the Wilderness roared with musketry. On his right, Getty was supposed to make contact with Crawford's division of Warren's embattled corps. But Crawford had marched north to support Warren, and Getty's men found the woods full of Confederates. Isolated and outnumbered, Getty's troops entrenched and steeled themselves for the onslaught.

General Lee wanted that crossroads too. During the day he had tacitly taken command of the troops on the Orange Plank road from Hill, whose illness was evident. Out in front, facing Getty's lines, he had a division led by Major General Henry Heth, who had fought with Braxton Bragg in Kentucky and had suffered a fractured skull at Gettysburg.

In the Wilderness, shortly a noon on May 5, Griffin's divisio Warren's V Corps attacked westw along the Orange Turnpike, rout Jones's brigade before being pus back by other elements of Ew corps. Farther south, Getty's F eral division, holding the in section of the Brock road and Orange Plank road, was attacke A. P. Hill's corps. When Getty reinforced by elements of Hanco II Corps, a stalemate ensu

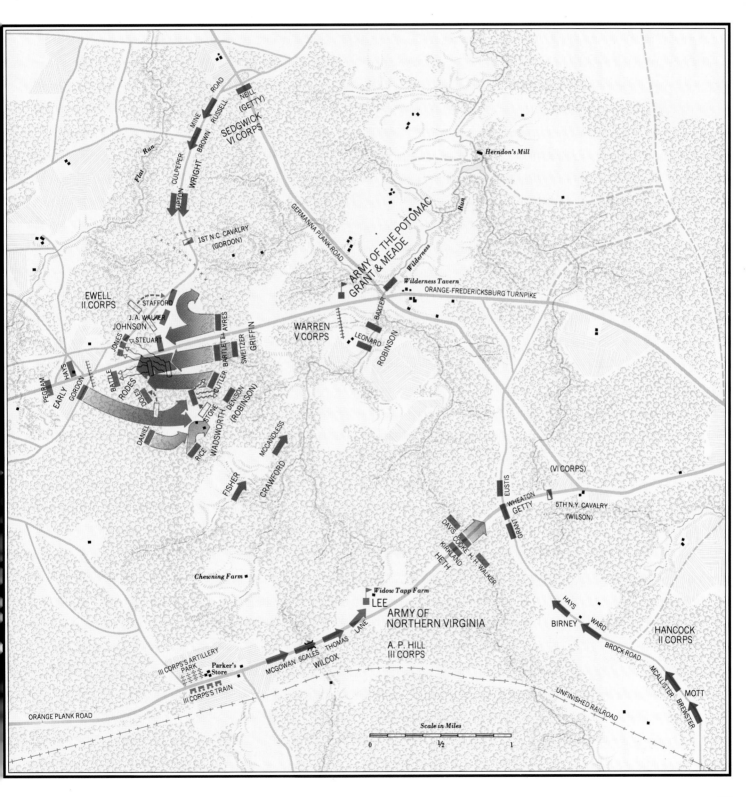

MINE ROAD

CULPEPER

WRIGHT

BROWN

RUSSELL

NEILL
(GETTY)

SEDGWICK
VI CORPS

Flat Run

UPTON

1ST N.C. CAVALRY
(GORDON)

GERMANNA PLANK ROAD

Herndon's Mill

ARMY OF THE POTOMAC
GRANT & MEADE

Wilderness Run

EWELL
II CORPS

STAFFORD

J. A. WALKER

JOHNSON

STEUART

JONES

BAXTER

Wilderness Tavern

ORANGE-FREDERICKSBURG TURNPIKE

AYRES

BARTLETT

SWEITZER

GRIFFIN

WARREN
V CORPS

LEONARD

ROBINSON

PEGRAM

EARLY

HAYS

GORDON

BATTLE

RODES

DOLES

OUTLER

STONE

DENISON
(ROBINSON)

DANIEL

RICE

WADSWORTH

McCANDLESS

FISHER

CRAWFORD

(VI CORPS)

EUSTIS

WHEATON

GETTY

GRANT

5TH N.Y. CAVALRY
(WILSON)

Chewning Farm

DAVIS

COOKE

H. H. WALKER

KIRKLAND

HETH

Widow Tapp Farm

LEE

ARMY OF
NORTHERN VIRGINIA

A. P. HILL
III CORPS

HAYS

WARD

BIRNEY

HANCOCK
II CORPS

III CORPS'S ARTILLERY
PARK

Parker's
Store

McGOWAN

SCALES

THOMAS

LANE

WILCOX

BROCK ROAD

McALLISTER

BREWSTER

III CORPS'S TRAIN

MOTT

ORANGE PLANK ROAD

UNFINISHED RAILROAD

Scale in Miles

0   ½   1

Hurrying from the burning battle-field, four Federals carry a wounded comrade in a blanket suspended from their muskets as some fellow soldiers nearby bear away another casualty on a stretcher. The artist, Alfred Waud, who drew this sketch on the scene, noted that many wounded died in the flames. "The fire advanced on all sides through the tall grass and, taking the dry pines, raged up to their tops."

Behind Heth was a second division, commanded by Major General Cadmus Marcellus Wilcox. Wilcox had been a friend of Ulysses Grant at West Point and a member of Grant's wedding 16 years before.

Slowly, Heth's vanguard pushed the Federals back. When Hancock arrived at the crossroads at 2 p.m., the first officer to reach him reported breathlessly, "Sir! General Getty is hard pressed and nearly out of ammunition."

"Tell him to hold on," Hancock shouted back, and directed his two lead divisions, commanded by Major General David Birney and Brigadier General Gershom Mott, to form up on Getty's left flank. It was no easy task. The Brock road was no better than the other lanes around it — narrow, hemmed in by forest and, by now, crowded with artillery and ordnance wagons that clogged the way.

Lee and A. P. Hill had stopped with their staffs at a clearing on the north side of the Orange Plank road about a mile behind the fighting. This spot was on the farm of a widow named Tapp. Lee saw that the place might be open enough for cannon and had Lieutenant Colonel William Poague, one of Hill's artillery commanders, post 12 guns along the west side of the field.

Lee was considering a full-scale attack on the crossroads. But he was worried about the gap on his left, two miles of snarled growth between Hill's corps and Ewell's. Lee ordered Wilcox's division to march across the Widow Tapp farm clearing and bridge the gap between Hill and Ewell. That left Heth, with about 7,000 Confederates, manning the Orange Plank road where Hancock was massing for an attack with 17,000 men.

About 4 p.m., Meade, growing impatient,

These twisted ramrods, found n the Orange Plank road long after battle, bear witness to the chaotic tensity of the fighting there. The m kets of some men grew so hot fr repeated firing that ignition occu even as they rammed a fresh ro home, sending the rod flying other cases, panic-stricken soldi simply forgot to withdraw the ra rods before pressing the trigg

ordered Getty to advance. Birney's division was to stay on his right while Mott remained on the left in reserve. When the time came to start, Birney and Mott were still struggling to get into position, and Getty moved out alone. Near the Turnpike, General Wadsworth received orders to move his wandering division south through the undergrowth — somehow — and pressure Hill's left.

Athwart the Orange Plank road, Heth's men had thrown up light breastworks on a thickly wooded rise overlooking a swampy hollow. The Confederates met Getty's attack with sheets of fire that staggered the Federals as they topped a low ridge 50 yards from the Confederate line. Getty's troops returned fire but could advance no farther. Just south of the pike, Getty's leftmost brigade, Vermont men under Colonel Lewis A. Grant, were hit on the flank by the Confederates. "As soon as the first volleys were over, our men hugged the ground as closely as possible and kept up a rapid fire," recalled Colonel Grant, "and the enemy did the same. The moment our men rose to advance, musketry cut them down with such slaughter that it was impracticable to do more than maintain our present position." Getty was stalled. He called for assistance, and soon reinforcements from Birney's division were struggling forward to shore up Getty's flanks.

After a hard march, Brigadier General Alexander Hays's brigade moved into position on Getty's right. Hays, a close friend of Grant and Hancock's, rode along his line, encouraging his men. Passing by his old regiment, the 63rd Pennsylvania, he stopped to speak. Just then a bullet struck him above the brim of his hat, and Hays fell from the saddle, mortally wounded.

At 5 p.m., Mott's division attacked — only to be routed and pushed back into its lines.

Although the Federal attack had stalled, Lee did not like the look of things and he sent a courier after Wilcox with orders to return to the Orange Plank road. Heth was going to need help. Indeed, Hancock was bringing his remaining two divisions, led by Brigadier Generals John Gibbon and Francis Barlow, into action, and the weight of Federal numbers was at last being felt. The fresh troops sprinted past Getty's exhausted men into the smoke-clouded forest, and the Confederate line shivered. But it did not quite break.

Wilcox returned and moved up to support Heth's flanks. Two of Wilcox's brigades under Brigadier Generals Samuel McGowan and Alfred M. Scales attacked south of the Orange Plank road, driving back the Federals and nearly capturing their supporting artillery before being driven back in turn by a Federal counterattack. Meanwhile, Lee sent his aide-de-camp, Colonel Charles Venable, forward to determine whether Hill's corps could hold on until darkness stopped the fighting. "If night would only come," implored Venable.

Every combatant prayed for darkness. But before it came, a courier reached A. P. Hill with the warning that a large Union force was approaching through the gap that Wilcox had abandoned. The only Confederate unit on hand to repel the Federals was a battalion of the 5th Alabama, which had been held back to guard the mushrooming clusters of prisoners. Hill, his ill health forgotten in the emergency, rounded up every noncombatant he could find and had them guard the prisoners. He faced the 125 Alabamians toward the woods and told them to charge, firing fast and giving the Rebel yell as though regiment after regiment were coming.

The approaching Federals were Wadsworth's men, who had been ordered from their position near the Orange Turnpike south to attack A. P. Hill's left. Wadsworth's troops were moving through brush so impenetrable that they could see no more than a few feet around them. The wild, screaming charge of the Alabamians rocked the Federals, stopped them in their tracks and riveted them in place. Soon night ended the Confederate attack. Wadsworth's troops rested fitfully in the thickets, their presence still menacing the Confederate flank.

To the north, meanwhile, the struggle along the Orange Turnpike had flared up once again. Wright's division of VI Corps had finally pushed its way down the tangled Culpeper Mine road and had taken position on Griffin's flank. At 3 p.m. Wright attacked — without results. Charges and countercharges surged for hours through the woodland, without conclusion.

As darkness descended, the noise of firing gave way all along the battle front to the sound of axes as men hastened to improvise breastworks. On the Turnpike, Major Abner Small of the 16th Maine was ordered to scout the woods in front of his position for stragglers. "I found a few," he reported. "They were badly frightened men, going they didn't know where, but anywhere away from that howling acre. I didn't blame them for dreading the return." Peering into the darkness, Major Small at one point "stumbled, fell, and my outflung hands pushed up a smoulder of leaves. The fire sprang into flame, caught in the hair and beard of a dead sergeant, and lighted a ghastly face and wide open eyes. I rushed away in horror."

The sounds of the wounded rose and fell in the darkness. Confederate Lieutenant McHenry Howard noted in his diary that "their moans and cries were painful to listen to. In the still night air every groan could be heard and the calls for water and entreaties to brothers and comrades by name to come and help them. Many, Federal and Confederate, lay within a dozen paces of our skirmish line, whom we found it impossible to succor, although we tried. I was myself fired on while making two separate efforts to get some in."

Most of the men in both armies, if they slept at all, simply nodded off at the spot where they had fired their last shot. The lines were a confused jumble, fronts askew, regiments and brigades scattered all over the tangled forest, not knowing whether their closest neighbors were friends or foes. Generals Heth and Wilcox were especially concerned about the state of their front, close as it was to Hancock's line. Their requests to realign their troops, however, were met by orders from A. P. Hill to "let the tired men rest." Tomorrow would be soon enough.

Both armies planned to attack early on May 6. General Meade was aware from prisoner interrogations that neither Longstreet nor Anderson had joined Lee. After conferring with Grant, Meade sent orders to Hancock to move at 5 a.m. to destroy A. P. Hill's divisions on the Orange Plank road before the outnumbered Confederates could be reinforced. Sedgwick and Warren were to engage Ewell along the Turnpike, making it impossible for Lee to draw men from that sector to help Hill.

By now Burnside's four divisions had crossed the Rapidan, and Grant ordered these fresh troops to advance into position before dawn. Burnside's lead division, commanded by Brigadier General Thomas G. Stevenson, was to march down the Brock road and join Hancock's corps on the Orange Plank road. Grant wanted the next two divisions, under Brigadier Generals Orlando B. Willcox and Robert B. Potter, to back up Wadsworth and penetrate the Wilderness gap that separated Lee's forces. Burnside's fourth division, under Brigadier General Edward Ferrero, was to guard the Germanna Plank road near the ford.

Lee, by his campfire at the Widow Tapp farm, pondered his advantages. Help was coming: Longstreet should arrive and be in position by morning, and Anderson's division was hurrying forward. Together they offered 20,000 of the Confederacy's best troops. Lee ordered Ewell to open up early and loud along the Turnpike to take some of the pressure off Hill's men, who would have to hold on until the reinforcements arrived.

Much depended on Longstreet's timing — and Burnside's. By 5 p.m. on May 5, Longstreet's men were within 10 miles of the front. He put them into bivouac with orders to move out again at 1 a.m. on the last leg. Lee had sent word for him to give up the Catharpin road and concentrate his advance on the Orange Plank road, the quicker to relieve Hill.

Ewell was the first to open fire as the sky east of the Wilderness turned red. Then Hancock, at 5 a.m., sent his skirmish lines forward to a spattering of musketry that signaled the dawn of a second violent day. With the charismatic Hancock spurring his men on, more than 20,000 Federals rumbled forward in three lines of battle on a front more than a mile long.

Wilcox's Confederates were the first to receive the shock. Still in disarray from the previous day's confusing maneuvers, they soon fell back; then many of them turned and ran. Wadsworth's men hit the left flank of Heth's line. Colonel William Martin of the 11th North Carolina dismally recalled that "our left flank rolled up as a sheet of paper would be rolled." Many of Heth's regiments, without waiting for the hammer to fall, retreated to form a new line. Colonel Theodore Lyman, riding to the scene as the fighting began, wrote that "two or three crashing volleys rang through the woods, and then the whole front was alive with musketry." Lyman found a jubilant Hancock at the crossroads. "We are driving them, sir," Hancock shouted. "Tell General Meade we are driving them most beautifully!"

Before 7 a.m., Hancock's blue host had moved forward a mile or more. Wadsworth's division, so befuddled the day before, was crashing in on the Federal right, and Stevenson's division was not too far behind. The Confederate front was dissolving. Some of Lee's men made a stand at the upper end of the Widow Tapp farm. Around them the remnants of Heth's and Wilcox's divisions marched to the rear.

As the Federal pressure mounted, Colonel Clark M. Avery of the 33rd North Carolina walked up and down his faltering line to encourage his men. They were lying down, and Avery made a good target. Major James A. Weston shouted, "Colonel, get down behind the breastworks. You will be killed if you walk about that way." Avery paid no heed. "We were compelled to retreat," recalled Weston. "I never saw Colonel Avery again."

Lee, in the clearing at the Widow Tapp farm, watched uncomfortably as his men emerged from the woods with the Union army close behind. For a time the only force

On the morning of May 6, Hancoc[k's] Federals seized the initiative, shatt[er]ing A. P. Hill's line across the Oran[ge] Plank road. Soon, however, Lo[ng]street's corps arrived from the w[est] and pushed the Federals back, [ad]vancing nearly to the Brock road [be]fore Longstreet was wounded arou[nd] noon. Lee launched a second assa[ult] against the Union left about 4 p.[m.] to no avail. A final advance by Jo[hn] Gordon's Confederate brigade on [the] Union right was stymied by darkne[ss] and the battle ended in stalema[te].

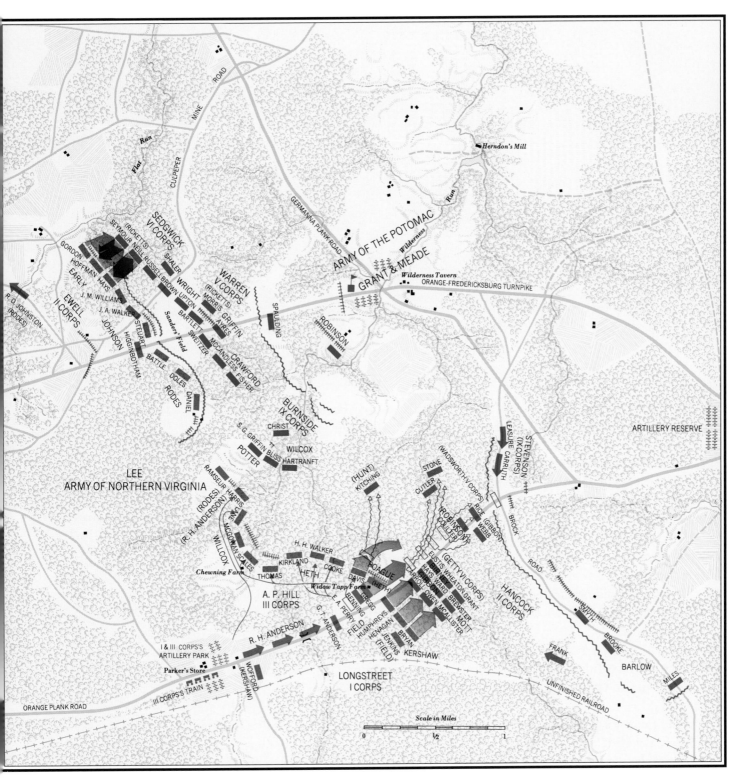

Herndon's Mill

Flat Run

MINE ROAD

CULPEPER

GERMANNA PLANK ROAD

Wilderness

ARMY OF THE POTOMAC

GRANT & MEADE

Wilderness Tavern

ORANGE-FREDERICKSBURG TURNPIKE

SEDGWICK
VI CORPS

GORDON
HOFFMAN
EARLY
HAYS
SEYMOUR
(RICKETT'S)
NEILL RUSSELL
BROWN
SHALER
UPTON
WRIGHT

J. M. WILLIAMS

J. A. WALKER

WARREN
V CORPS

(RICKETT'S)
MORRIS
AYRES
GRIFFIN

BARTLETT
SWEITZER
McCANDLESS
CRAWFORD
LYSTER

SPAULDING

ROBINSON

EWELL
II CORPS

R. D. JOHNSTON
(RODES)

JOHNSON

HIGGINBOTHAM

STEUART

Sander's Field

BATTLE
DOLES
DANIEL
RODES

BURNSIDE
IX CORPS

ARTILLERY RESERVE

S. G. GRIFFIN
CHRIST
BLISS
WILCOX
HARTRANFT

POTTER

LEE
ARMY OF NORTHERN VIRGINIA

RAMSEUR
HARRIS
(RODES)
DANE
(R. H. ANDERSON)
McGOWAN
SCALES

WILCOX

Chewning Farm

THOMAS

KIRKLAND
H. H. WALKER
COOKE
DAVIS

A. P. HILL
III CORPS

HETH

Widow Tapp Farm

POAGUE
(HETH)

(HUNT)
KITCHING

STONE

CUTLER

(WADSWORTH V CORPS)

RICE

ROBINSON
COULTER

(GETTY VI CORPS)

EUSTIS
WHEATON
GRANT

WEBB
(GIBBON)

STEVENSON
(IX CORPS)

LEASURE CARRUTH

BROCK

ROAD

GREGG

E. A. PERRY
FIELD
BENNING
G. T. ANDERSON

R. H. ANDERSON

I & III CORPS'S
ARTILLERY PARK

Parker's Store

WOFFORD
(KERSHAW)

III CORPS'S TRAIN

ORANGE PLANK ROAD

LONGSTREET
I CORPS

HUMPHREYS
HENAGAN

JENKINS
(FIELD)

KERSHAW

CARROLL OWEN
HAYS WARD
BREWSTER
McALLISTER
MOTT

BRYAN

HANCOCK
II CORPS

SMYTH

BROOKE

FRANK

BARLOW

MILES

UNFINISHED RAILROAD

Scale in Miles

0   ½   1

75

that held this clearing was the 12 guns commanded by Colonel William Poague, the 28-year-old Virginian. Poague bought precious time, staggering Wadsworth's Federals with blasts of canister. Nevertheless, Lee, standing behind the guns, perceived a disaster in the making. He ordered his wagons made ready for immediate withdrawal. Then his slow temper flared. He called to Brigadier General Samuel McGowan of Wilcox's division, "Is this splendid brigade of yours running like a flock of geese?" In truth, the men were not panicked.

"General," answered McGowan evenly, "these men are not whipped. They only want a place to form and they will fight as well as they ever did."

Now the elements of the Wilderness took their toll on the Federal juggernaut. Having become disoriented in the thickets, Wads-worth's troops sliced to the Orange Plank road at an angle, inadvertently forcing Birney's men — Hancock's lead division — off the road to the left. Regiments and brigades became hopelessly entangled and, just as a glorious victory seemed within reach, Hancock's offensive began to falter. Burnside's two divisions in the center were having as much trouble making their way through the undergrowth as their comrades had had the day before. They were hours away from being able to offer help.

At this pivotal moment Longstreet appeared, his corps striding up the Orange Plank road in parallel columns with Major General Charles W. Field's division on the left and Brigadier General Joseph B. Kershaw's on the right. Longstreet's men shouldered their way through the wreckage of Hill's corps and formed to take up the fight.

In a view from the rear of their line, troops of Wadsworth's Federal division load and fire on the Confederates in the woods by the Orange Plank road on May 6. A Federal officer reported ruefully that after Wadsworth was mortally wounded, much of the division bolted for the rear, "and upon getting out of the woods halted and proceeded to make coffee."

No one was happier to see them than Lee. As Brigadier General John Gregg of Field's division was leading his men past Poague's guns, Lee, riding Traveller, reined up beside him. "General," asked Lee, " what brigade is this?"

"The Texas Brigade," responded Gregg.

"Hurrah for Texas," shouted Lee, his famous composure abandoned. He took off his hat and waved it. "Go and drive out these people."

"Attention, Texas Brigade!" Gregg ordered. "The eyes of General Lee are upon you. Forward . . . march!"

Standing in his stirrups, Lee watched with his hat held aloft. "Texans always move them," he said.

Then Lee, with reckless enthusiasm, began to ride forward with the Texans. "Lee to the rear," the men shouted. "General Lee, go back." He seemed not to hear them. Only after several men had broken ranks to turn Lee's horse around did the commanding general agree to ride behind their line. He was still in danger. Longstreet later recalled that he rode up and, seeing Lee "off his balance," promised the commanding general that "his line would be recovered in an hour if he would permit me to handle the troops." Otherwise, Longstreet told Lee with affectionate bluntness, "I would like to ride to some place of safety, as it is not quite comfortable where we are."

Lee reluctantly sought cover and Longstreet proceeded with his attack. Gregg's 800 Texans advanced through the woods "with apparently resistless force," recalled one of Longstreet's officers. The Federals fought back fiercely, and within 10 minutes nearly half of the Texans were casualties, including Gregg, who was badly wounded. Two more of Longstreet's brigades followed the Texans, driving the Federals back in confusion. Longstreet meanwhile hurled two of Kershaw's brigades down the Orange Plank road, and all along Hancock's right the tired and disorganized Federals were forced to withdraw. Hancock, his ebullience fading, sent a somber dispatch to Meade: "They are pressing us on the road a good deal. If more force were here now, I could use it."

Hancock also was having problems on his left. He had entrusted the protection of that flank to his left wing commander, Brigadier General John Gibbon, a twice-wounded professional who fought for the Union even though his three brothers were fighting for the South. Gibbon had kept Brigadier General Francis Barlow's division and most of II Corps's artillery deployed on an open stretch of high ground along the Brock road about a mile south of the Orange Plank road intersection. As the rest of the corps advanced, a gap opened between Birney's troops and those of Barlow. As early as 7 a.m. Hancock had sent a message to Gibbon, ordering him to send Barlow's troops forward to attack the Confederate right. Gibbon would insist forever that he never got the message. He did send one of Barlow's brigades forward, but he held the rest of the force in place that morning, expecting a full-scale attack at any moment from the south.

By midmorning Longstreet had almost driven Hancock's command back to its starting place; and soon the blue and the gray had fought themselves to a stalemate.

But Longstreet had been alerted to the gap between Birney and Barlow in the left of Hancock's line. Brigadier General Martin L. Smith, Lee's chief engineer, had made a personal reconnaissance and found a hidden route — the bed of an unfinished railroad — that led right into it. Longstreet ordered his adjutant, Lieutenant Colonel G. Moxley Sorrel, to take four brigades along the railroad cut and advance north, attacking Birney's exposed flank. At 11 a.m. the Confederates moved out unseen, and then they burst from the brambles, yelling as they came. The closest Federals, men of Colonel Robert McAllister's brigade, were hit before they could change front to face the attackers, and they retreated in disorder. Then more of the Federal troops fell back, fighting, and the Union left was close to collapse. When the commanders met years later, Hancock would tell Longstreet, "You rolled me up like a wet blanket."

On Hancock's right, General James Wadsworth was working hard to rally his division. By now 1,100 of his 5,000 men were

casualties. The troops were falling back, not in panic but, as one officer said, "as though they had fought all they meant to fight for the present." Wadsworth ordered the 20th Massachusetts to attack directly down the Orange Plank road. Soon the 20th's Colonel George N. Macy fell with a shattered foot and had to pass command over to Major Henry Abbott. Within moments, Abbott fell mortally wounded. Wadsworth was riding with the Massachusetts men. Suddenly his horse bolted forward into the Confederate line and he took a bullet to the head. Wadsworth fell mortally wounded from his horse, surrounded by Confederates who took him back to their own field hospital. The 20th Massachusetts, having suffered 140 casualties, retreated. By 12:30 p.m. the Confederate momentum had slowed, allowing Hancock's battered Federals to withdraw behind their earthworks.

Longstreet was riding along the Orange Plank road with his officers, planning a follow-up attack. At his side rode Brigadier General Micah Jenkins, a 28-year-old South Carolinian and one of the most able young officers in the Army of Northern Virginia. Jenkin's brigade was to lead the new assault.

All at once rifles opened up from the woods to the right. Troops of Brigadier General William Mahone's brigade of Virginians were firing down the road at Confederate troops they mistakenly thought were the enemy. Longstreet and his party were in the line of that fire.

"Friends!" shouted General Joseph Kershaw. "We are friends."

The firing stopped, but the damage had been done. A courier and a staff captain had been killed instantly. Jenkins took a bullet to the brain. Major John C. Haskell, one

An avid young warrior who first distinguished himself in the fighting around Richmond in 1862, Brigadier General Micah Jenkins welcomed the chance to assault Hancock's Federals on May 6, assuring a fellow officer as they rode forward: "We shall smash them now." Moments later Jenkins lay mortally wounded, cut down by an errant Confederate volley that also felled James Longstreet.

of Longstreet's staff officers, remembered that as Jenkins was being carried away "he would cheer his men and implore them to sweep the enemy into the river." He would live only a few hours. Longstreet, too, had been hit. "At the moment that Jenkins fell," he wrote later, "I received a severe shock from a minie ball passing through my throat and right shoulder. The blow lifted me from the saddle, and my right arm dropped to my side, but I settled back to my seat and started to ride on, when in a minute the flow of blood admonished me that my work for the day was done. As I turned to ride back, members of the staff, seeing me about to fall,

dismounted and lifted me to the ground."

Longstreet was placed on a litter and carried to the rear. His hat was over his face, to shield him from the sun. The wounded general could hear the men murmuring along the line: "He is dead, and they are telling us he is only wounded." Wanting to reassure them, Longstreet recalled, "I raised my hat with my left hand." A cheer went up. "The burst of voices and the flying of hats in the air eased my pain somewhat."

Almost exactly a year earlier, in the same cursed woods and in similar circumstances, Stonewall Jackson had fallen. But Longstreet's chief medical officer pronounced his wound "not necessarily mortal." The "Old Warhorse" would recover. For now, Lee took over his command.

At 3 p.m. there was a lull in the fighting. On his headquarters stump near the crossroads, Grant was still whittling and smoking. Earlier, when told of Hancock's reversal, his quiet response had been to throw more troops into the melee. "Feeding the fight," his staff called it.

In early afternoon, Grant scheduled a coordinated attack against Longstreet and Hill along the Orange Plank road. It was to commence at 6 p.m. But Lee struck first. Shortly after 4 p.m. he sent Hill's and Longstreet's troops forward in a concentrated assault on Hancock's line.

Hancock's divisions were waiting behind their breastworks along the Brock road. During the lull, their flank had been shored —Burnside had moved in on the right. As the Confederates attacked, brush fires broke out again on the battlefield; the grayclad men moved past little patches of flame as they advanced into raking rifle volleys and artillery fire from Hancock's breastworks. The

wind was in their favor, blowing from west to east. Soon the breastworks themselves caught fire. Federal soldiers pulled back, choking on the smoke, and in places Federal and Confederate were no more than a dozen paces apart, firing at each other through sheets of flame.

Anderson's Georgians and South Carolinians of Colonel John Henagan's brigade reached the burning earthworks in Gershom Mott's front and planted their flags in the face of devastating artillery fire. But Hancock had reserves to send in, among them Colonel Sprigg Carroll's brigade — veterans of Gettysburg. Carroll's men recaptured the length of breastwork and plugged the hole, while suffering great losses. Carroll himself was wounded for the second time in two days. Burnside's two divisions joined in and held their own, if no more.

After an hour of fighting, the Confederate offensive had been stymied. A smoldering no man's land littered with bodies separated the two armies as the shooting slowed. There was no possibility now of the Union attack that Grant had ordered.

Lee, in frustration, rode north to where Ewell was holding his position astride the Turnpike. "Cannot something be done on this flank?" he asked.

The answer was yes. Brigadier General John Gordon, whose Georgians manned the Confederate far left, had been convinced since morning that his line overlapped that of the Federals to his front, making them vulnerable to a flanking attack. He had scouted the area himself to confirm his conviction that the enemy flank was in the air. At first Ewell had refused Gordon's requests to attack; but after making a reconnaissance of his own, he changed his mind.

Lee liked the idea. He saw a chance to

Confederates momentarily gain the smoldering Federal breastworks along the Brock road in a misdated sketch showing the high point of Lee's assault late on May 6. "A better charge, or more determined, I never saw," one of the defenders conceded. "At some points the timber used in the earthworks was fired, and our men had to stand back out of the line of flame and shoot through it at the Confederates."

repeat the devastating surprise flank attack that he and Stonewall Jackson had accomplished against Joseph Hooker at Chancellorsville a year earlier. So about 6 p.m. Gordon's Georgians moved forward, supported by Brigadier General Robert Johnston's brigade. As the fighting developed, Early would throw in additional troops.

The Union right flank was John Sedgwick's responsibility, and throughout the day he had ignored the possibility of an attack. To make matters worse, the troops there were among his least dependable: two brigades that had been led to defeat so often by a previous commander, Major General Robert Milroy, that they had become known as "Milroy's weary boys." Between them and the Rapidan stretched several miles of unoccupied country. From this unexpected direction, the Georgians struck with a whoop, and the weary boys broke and fled.

Soon fleeing soldiers were rushing past Sedgwick's headquarters. He sent for reinforcements and galloped toward the fighting. Shortly, a few officers reached Meade and Grant's campsite, spouting tales of disaster: The entire VI Corps was collapsing, Sedgwick himself had been captured. All was lost. "Nonsense!" bellowed Meade. "If they have broken our lines, they can do nothing more tonight."

Grant was also told of the Confederate flank attack. A panicky officer approached him, predicting that Lee was throwing his entire force between them and the river, cutting the Union army off. Retreat was imperative. Grant, usually so phlegmatic, replied with an outburst that matched Meade's. Horace Porter, Grant's aide, later wrote that Grant sputtered: "I am tired of hearing about what Lee is going to do. Some of you always seem to think he is suddenly going to turn a double somersault and land in our rear and on both of our flanks at the same time. Go back to your command and try to think about what we are going to do ourselves, instead of what Lee is going to do."

Darkness and Federal reinforcements put an end to Gordon's attack. The Georgians had inflicted about 400 casualties and had captured several hundred men, including the commanders of the two hapless brigades on the Federal far right, Brigadier Generals Alexander Shaler and Truman Seymour.

Even General Sedgwick had a narrow escape. A Confederate officer had leveled a pistol at him at close range and ordered him to surrender — just before the Confederate himself was shot down.

Robert E. Lee rode back to his headquarters at the Widow Tapp farm. In the woods the moans of the wounded turned to screams as fire engulfed them. Paper cartridges in their pockets or in cartridge boxes ignited and exploded with an eerie clatter. In two days of fighting, by some counts, Lee's army had sustained a minimum of 7,500 casualties. The general put the survivors to work strengthening their defenses.

Shortly after dark, Ulysses Grant offered George Meade the last cigar in his pocket and sought the privacy of his tent. The action in the Wilderness had cost Grant's Army of the Potomac 17,666 men killed, wounded or captured. Before retiring, he had a word for a correspondent who was about to depart for Washington to file his story on the battle. "If you see the President," said Grant, "tell him, from me, that whatever happens, there will be no turning back."

A Slaughter at the Crossroads

Fog, smoke, and the loathsome stench of burned and decaying flesh hung over the Wilderness on Saturday morning, May 7. So did an eerie calm, bewildering after the violence of the last two days. There were sporadic bursts of musket fire, signaling brief encounters between Federal and Confederate skirmishers, and a few cannon shots, but veterans — their ears attuned to the ominous roar that indicated the start of a real battle — shrugged off these noises as meaningless clatter. Slowly the troops on both sides realized that neither of the commanding generals was inclined to renew the carnage in the desolate forest.

General Lee briefly entertained the notion that Grant might be about to disengage and withdraw eastward, following the long train of ambulances that the Confederates could see snaking toward Fredericksburg. Another alternative for Grant was a retreat north, back across the Rapidan. The fact that Grant had not attacked at first light seemed to indicate that he was contemplating a move, but in what direction?

For Grant, there was only one choice. At 6:30 a.m. he had written an order that was soon delivered to General Meade. It began: "Make all preparations during the day for a night march to take position at Spotsylvania Court House with one corps" — a move not to the north or east, but to the southeast, a dozen miles closer to Richmond. Grant was not going to retreat. Despite the heavy losses in the Wilderness, he would continue to press the enemy.

Grant had chosen Spotsylvania as his immediate objective for several reasons. It was an important crossroads that lay on the route from the Wilderness to Hanover Junction, where Lee's principal supply lines met — the Richmond, Fredericksburg & Potomac and the Virginia Central Railroads. And it was the logical target if Grant meant to slip by Lee's right flank. Should the Federals reach Spotsylvania first, they would be astride the best route to Richmond and Lee would be forced either to attack Grant's larger army or to lead a desperate race on inferior roads to reach a blocking position and protect the Confederate capital.

Grant's orders to Meade were, as usual, clear and specific. General Warren's V Corps would march south on the Brock road, passing behind General Hancock's men in their charred and smoking breastworks. Hancock's troops would hold their position, covering the army's shift southward, and then follow Warren. John Sedgwick and his VI Corps would head for Chancellorsville and turn south. General Ambrose Burnside was to follow Sedgwick. If the movement went as planned, Warren's vanguard would be at Spotsylvania early the next morning, May 8, digging trenches and preparing to meet any troops Lee might send in pursuit.

Before Grant's flanking march began, parties of Federal troops emerged from their

J. R. Montgomery of the 11th Mississippi, mortally wounded at Spotsylvania on May 10, used the last of his strength to write this poignant letter to his father. As his hand grew shaky and his blood stained the page, Montgomery knew the end was near. "May we meet in heaven," he wrote, closing with the words, "Your Dying Son, J. R. Montgomery."

lines to recover the wounded that could be reached and to bury the dead. Confederates, also taking advantage of the lull, performed the same sad chores, often interring blue-clad corpses. "At one place in front of the Third Brigade," wrote John Casler of the 33rd Virginia, "where the enemy had made a desperate charge on the 6th, we buried 500 of them that lay in line as they fell." As the Confederates buried the dead, Casler admitted, they rifled the corpses for supplies. "We got out of rations during this battle and could not get to our wagons, but the Yankees had four or five days rations of hard tack and bacon in their haversacks, and we would get them from the dead. I have been so hungry that I have cut the blood off from crackers and eaten them."

All day ambulances rolled away from the Union line, but when night and the time to march approached, scores of wounded still lay uncollected. "As we loaded ambulances and army wagons to their utmost capacity,"

surgeon George Stevens wrote, "making a train of many miles in extent, some two hundred wounded of our VI Corps were left upon the ground. It was, indeed, a sickening thought."

During the day, reports of Federal cavalry activity to the southeast persuaded Lee that Grant was about to move and that Spotsylvania was his destination. For insurance Lee had ordered a rough track cut through the forest, connecting his right on the Orange Plank road to a branch of the Catharpin road that gave access to Spotsylvania. It would give him the shortest route for a covering march to the courthouse. Then when some of A. P. Hill's staff officers informed Lee that, using a telescope, they had seen guns being moved to the Federal left, the Confederate commander was convinced.

Clearly a race was on. Lee ordered Richard Anderson, who had taken over for the wounded James Longstreet, to ready two divisions for a night march toward Spotsylvania. Anderson, holding the Confederate right, was in the best position for this side slip. Richard Ewell and A. P. Hill would follow with their corps as soon as they were certain that the enemy trenches on their fronts were empty.

Anderson, figuring he had 11 miles to cover, set his starting time for 11 p.m. The Federals were on the move well before that. Around 8:30 that night, Grant and his staff made for the Brock road to ride with Warren's vanguard. Warren's men, pulled from their positions and told to march, did not know at first whether they were advancing or retreating. Progress was even more difficult than usual. The road was dry and the dust was choking. Smoky fires still sputtered nearby and that smell was everywhere. The men were forced to halt and stand aside as ambulances rattled past. Hancock's troops, sprawled by the road trying to sleep, presented an obstacle course in the dark.

Then came a call "Give way to the right!" and a small cavalcade was let through, Grant in the lead on Cincinnati, riding south. The men grasped what this meant and, despite orders to be as quiet as possible, gave a great cheer, tossing their hats as they yelled. The big horse grew excited and reared. When Grant got the animal under control, he told his staff to hush the men lest the Confederates hear. Nevertheless, "a great burst of cheering," a Maine boy wrote, greeted Grant wherever "he rode swiftly and silently by." The agony of the Wilderness was not to be wasted after all. "Our spirits rose," one veteran recalled. "That night we were happy."

The Confederates heard the cheering, of course, as well as the tramp of thousands of feet. They, too, had been admonished to maintain silence: "No fires or noise or any unusual signs, such as rattling canteens or metal," Lieutenant McHenry Howard recalled. But like the Federals, the Confederates were jubilant. They assumed the Federals were in retreat and looked upon the Wilderness as a victory. As they moved down the stump-studded, fresh-cut road, some of Anderson's men cried out, "Three cheers for General Lee!" The result, Captain James F. J. Caldwell of the 1st South Carolina later said, was "the grandest vocal exhibition" he had ever heard. One brigade after another let out the Rebel yell until "it went echoing to the remotest corner of Ewell's corps." Three times "this mighty wave of sound rang along the Confederate lines. The effect was beyond expression. It seemed to fill every heart with new life, to inspire every nerve with might never known before."

The yelling over, Anderson's men stumbled on down the crude road through the woods. The troops badly needed a rest, but as Anderson recalled, "I found the woods in every direction on fire and burning furiously, and there was no suitable place for rest." So he kept his troops going.

The equally weary Federals were having their own problems moving on the clogged Brock road — and the delays almost cost them their lieutenant general. As Grant and his party approached Todd's Tavern late at night, they decided to take a lane to the right rather than struggle through the crowds of troops up ahead. Lieutenant Colonel Cyrus B. Comstock, Grant's staff engineer, soon sensed they were going in the wrong direction. Riding ahead, Comstock saw Anderson's Confederate infantry crossing the lane a couple of hundred yards away. Comstock spurred back to his commander, urging him to turn around immediately or risk becoming a prisoner of war. An annoyed Grant reluctantly reversed Cincinnati and, reaching Todd's Tavern at midnight, slept on the ground under his overcoat.

Despite the wrong turn, Grant reached Todd's Tavern ahead of Warren's infantrymen, who had been moving all too slowly through the darkness. "The road was literally jammed with troops," Artillery Colonel Charles Wainwright recalled. "Never before did I see such slow progress made." In fact, some of the delay was the fault of the Union army's own cavalry.

Earlier that day, two divisions of Philip Sheridan's horsemen, having bested General Jeb Stuart's cavalry in a sharp clash at Todd's Tavern, had blithely bivouacked by the side of the road south of the tavern. Sheridan intended that the troopers ride the next morning, May 8, to block the bridges across the Po River, heading off any of Lee's units that were Spotsylvania bound. But Anderson's troops had been marching hard, and they would reach the most important of the spans, Block House Bridge, at daybreak.

General Meade, arriving at Todd's Tavern after midnight with the head of Warren's column, was outraged to find Federal cavalry

Federal soldiers cheer General Grant *(center, on horseback)* for his decision to press on toward Richmond rather than withdraw after the Battle of the Wilderness. Grant was not pleased by the noisy accolade so close to the Confederate lines: "This is most unfortunate," he said. "The sound will reach the ears of the enemy, and I fear it may reveal our movement."

sleeping up ahead. Riding forward, he angrily ordered Sheridan's two division commanders, Brigadier Generals Wesley Merritt and David Gregg, to clear out and ride southward. "It is of the utmost importance that not the slightest delay occur in your opening the Brock Road beyond Spotsylvania Court House," Meade said, "as an infantry corps is now on the way to occupy the place."

Despite Meade's peremptory order, Warren's infantry found their march stalled by a sea of Federal troopers jamming the Brock road as they prepared to move out. The foot soldiers were ordered to close up and halt — and quickly fell asleep in the road. It was 6 a.m. before Warren could get his men moving again. As they started, they heard carbine fire far ahead.

The distant firing signaled the beginning of the Battle of Spotsylvania. Like many of history's great battles, it began with a series of accidental engagements as opposing units blundered into each other.

The first shooting occurred at the crossroads itself, where yet another division of Sheridan's cavalry, led by Brigadier General James Wilson, clashed with Brigadier General Thomas Rosser's cavalry brigade. Then Wesley Merritt's horsemen, urged down the Brock road by Meade, ran head on into a blocking force of Confederate cavalry commanded by General Lee's nephew, Major General Fitzhugh Lee, about two miles short of the courthouse.

Jeb Stuart immediately sent a courier to General Lee, asking for reinforcements. En route the messenger encountered General Anderson's division. Anderson's column of weary infantrymen had completed the worst of their exhausting march, outdistancing Warren's Federals in the nightlong race

General Richard (Fighting Dick) Anderson, whose troops beat the Federals in the race to the Spotsylvania Court House, was one of the South's most popular commanders. When he replaced the wounded Longstreet as corps commander, Anderson's new men tossed their hats into the air, moving the general to tears.

southward. The Confederates were just falling in to continue across the undefended Block House Bridge when Stuart's messenger galloped up. Anderson sent one brigade along the Brock road to help Fitzhugh Lee hold off Merritt's troopers. He then ordered a second brigade to march to the relief of Rosser's men, who had been driven out of Spotsylvania by Wilson's Federals.

Merritt, meanwhile, had called for aid from Warren's approaching corps. Warren sent Brigadier General John Robinson's division down the Brock road to a clearing on the farm of a family named Alsop. It was already "broad day and scorching hot when we reached the cleared lands of the Alsop farm," recalled Abner Small of the 16th Maine. "We were fully two miles from where we had first deployed; our men had run a part of the way, and many had dropped out, overcome by heat and weariness."

Robinson and his two leading brigades were in for an unpleasant surprise. Thinking they were attacking only a relatively small if stubborn line of dismounted Confederate cavalry, they found themselves instead facing furious volleys from a brigade of Anderson's infantry. "Fire, deadening fire, is

Confederate General Henry (Mud) Walker, who had been wounded twice at Gaines's Mill in 1862, was again wounded during the battle for Spotsylvania. This time the 31-year-old general lost a foot and had to be relieved of command — at considerable cost to the Confederate cause.

poured into that column by our men," a South Carolinian later wrote. General Robinson himself was among the first to go down, badly wounded in the left knee. His troops were bloodily repulsed, and they retreated back across the clearing. The exhausted Federal survivors found they did not have the strength to run back to safety; they could only stumble to the rear.

Meade, establishing his headquarters two miles east of Todd's Tavern, initially refused to believe that Confederate infantry had beaten Warren's corps to Spotsylvania. But as the morning wore on and Warren's tired regiments were unable to dent the improvised Confederate line, Meade realized that he was facing more than cavalry. By noon Meade had received word from Warren that the Federal attacks were hopelessly stalled and that reinforcements were needed. Meade immediately ordered Sedgwick's corps to form on Warren's left, then directed that combined attack be made "with vigor and without delay."

Again Meade would be frustrated, however. Sedgwick could not get in position until 5 p.m. By then Ewell's 17,000 men were coming in on Anderson's right. The Federal assault was ill-coordinated and halfhearted; like those that had gone before, it ended in failure. With Ewell's troops now extending and strengthening Lee's defensive line, the Confederates were simply too strong for the dog-tired Federal attackers. When darkness ended the firing for the day, Meade's route to Spotsylvania remained blocked.

The Confederates spent the hot morning of May 9 digging, strengthening their earthworks by the hour and waiting for the attack. "The neighboring fences were robbed," James Caldwell, the South Carolinian, remembered, "and the rails piled up before us. Earth was then thrown over these, from the inner side, so that by night we had a pretty good trench and breastwork to cover us."

While the Confederates dug in, Meade and Grant were busy deploying their forces for battle. Three of Hancock's divisions marched cross-country from Todd's Tavern to take up positions on Warren's right. Sedgwick's corps took Warren's left and entrenched. Beyond Sedgwick, Burnside was moving under orders to swing out and come at Spotsylvania from the northeast. Sheridan was ordered to take most of the Cavalry Corps southward, engage Stuart's troopers and cut Lee's supply lines.

With Ewell's corps, Lee had extended Anderson's right on a northeast slant. A. P. Hill's corps — now commanded by Major General Jubal Early because Hill was so sick he could not even sit up — moved into line of battle along Ewell's right rear. By 4 p.m. the Confederate front resembled a ragged *V*, the flanks bent back to meet attacks from either left or right and a strong salient in the center, protruding northward. Much of Lee's position, situated on a curving ridge and screened by trees and undergrowth, was dif-

Union General John Sedgwick, killed instantly by a sniper's bullet, lies surrounded by his grief-stricken staff. Major Charles Whittier cradles the general's head while Captain Richard Halstead feels vainly for a pulse and two officers signal for assistance. Crouching next to Whittier is Major Thomas Hyde, who later wrote of Sedgwick as a cherished friend whose "noble heart was stilled at last."

ficult for Federal officers to discern, and Confederate skirmishers kept up a sniping fire on anyone who showed himself along the Federal lines.

One of these snipers dealt the Army of the Potomac a costly blow. "Uncle John" Sedgwick was overseeing the placement of some artillery in his corps's forward lines. Trying to reassure his men, who were unnerved by the Confederate sharpshooters, he said in jest that "they couldn't hit an elephant at this distance." Just then a bullet slammed into Sedgwick's face below the left eye. His stunned staff rushed to Sedgwick's side, but could do nothing for him. After twice asking "Is he really dead?" Grant pronounced the loss as costly as that of a division. "Never had such a gloom rested upon the whole army on account of the death of one man as came over it when the heavy tidings passed along the lines that General Sedgwick was killed," wrote surgeon George Stevens of Sedgwick's corps. General Horatio Wright replaced Sedgwick as commander of VI Corps.

Grant spent the afternoon of May 9 searching for a soft spot in Lee's lines. His most promising probe was directed at the Confederate left. Hancock crossed the meandering Po River with three divisions and advanced south toward Block House Bridge, intending to cross the river again there and circle eastward around the exposed left flank of Anderson's corps.

Dense woods slowed Hancock's advance, however, and dark came before his men could reach the bridge. The next morning II Corps skirmishers found Brigadier General William Mahone's Confederate brigade blocking the way on the far bank. Nevertheless, Hancock adroitly slipped a brigade commanded by Colonel John Brooke farther

south and across the river well in Mahone's rear. Now Lee was in trouble, his position turned and his communications threatened. If Brooke's lone brigade could be reinforced quickly and heavily, Lee would be forced to abandon his trenches.

Unfortunately for the Army of the Potomac, Grant failed to appreciate the opening Hancock and Brooke had provided. Knowing that Mahone had been detached to extend the Confederate left flank, Grant assumed that the Confederate line must have been weakened elsewhere. He busily set to work planning a frontal attack, proposed by General Warren, on Anderson's main works. Giving Warren a free rein, Grant and Meade recalled two of Hancock's divisions from the far right to assist.

But Warren failed completely to break the Confederate line. Only a few of his troops reached the Confederate entrenchments, and they were killed or driven back. Three hours later the assault was renewed and was again repulsed. The Federals had been committed piecemeal, and the two fruitless attacks cost them about 3,000 men.

The Federals saw another chance farther to the east. There, Horatio Wright had made a reconnaissance and concluded that the salient in the center of the Confederate positions — called the Mule Shoe by its defenders — was a vulnerable spot. To assault it, Wright called on one of his most brilliant young officers, a freckled 24-year-old colonel and West Point graduate named Emory Upton. A brigade commander in Wright's VI Corps, Upton had been preaching a new theory of attack — a hammer blow by a concentrated striking force advancing on a much narrower front than usual. Once this force had shattered a small segment of the enemy's line, a second wave of attackers would pour through the gap and strike the beleaguered Confederates in flank and rear. To Upton's mind, that was the way to crack those solid Confederate defenses. Wright decided to test Upton's theory, giving him 12 veteran infantry regiments totaling roughly 5,000 men to use as his hammer.

Upton's objective was formidable. The Mule Shoe bristled with artillery and was shielded by a heavy abatis of felled trees, their branches sharpened and pointed toward the attackers. The main trench line,

built up with logs and banked earth, was the strongest constructed thus far by Lee's forces. At right angles to this line ran traverses, mounds of earth that extended rearward and protected the defenders against enfilade fire. And 100 yards to the rear of the principal breastworks Ewell was building a second set of defenses.

Upton's men for their part would have one advantage: Advancing from the northeast, they would be hidden by thick pine woods until they got to within 200 yards of Ewell's forward trenches. They would charge across

General Gouverneur K. Warren, in command of the Federal V Corps, gallantly rallies a broken brigade for another assault on Anderson's Confederate line on May 10. Warren is tenaciously clutching the shortened staff of his tattered corps flag, which a moment earlier had been shot in two in his hands.

those 200 yards, with bayonets fixed. It was pointless, Upton believed, to stop and shoot while moving over open ground swept by both canister and rifle fire. Only speed would effect a breach. The men, therefore, would not open fire until they had arrived at the enemy works.

Upton formed the troops into a compact mass, four lines deep, three regiments side by side in each line. The first line was to cross the Confederate earthworks and then split up, the 5th Maine swinging left, the 121st New York and the 96th Pennsylvania turning right, to capture a Confederate battery. The second line would dash through the gap and head for Ewell's backup trenches. The third and fourth lines were to go into action wherever more Federal pressure was needed. If the plan was successful, Upton's novel assault would produce a narrow but deep fissure in the Confederate defenses. If the hole could be widened, Lee's entire front might collapse.

Shortly before 6 p.m. Federal batteries opened fire, and at 6:10 Upton gave the order to charge. The defenders in the Mule Shoe were cooking what Artillery Lieutenant Robert Stiles called their "mean and meager little rations." Then, Stiles wrote, "someone rose up, and looking over the works — it was shading down a little toward the dark — cried out: 'Hello! What's this? Why, here come our men on the run from — no, by heavens! It's the Yankees!'"

Within five minutes, the swiftest men in Upton's three leading regiments had made it through the tangled abatis to the parapet of the earthworks. "The first of our men who tried to surmount the works fell pierced through the head by musket-balls," Upton recalled. "Others, seeing the fate of their comrades, held their pieces at arms length and fired downward, while others, poising their pieces vertically, hurled them down upon their enemy, pinning them to the ground." Upton reported that the Confederate troops, part of Brigadier General George Doles's Georgia brigade, "absolutely refused to yield the ground." But their stand did not last long. "Numbers prevailed," Upton wrote, "and, like a resistless wave, the column poured over the works."

As more and more Federals got into the trenches, the Georgia troops broke and ran for the second line, which also gave way. The gap, meanwhile, was being widened by more waves of Upton's attackers. The plan had worked so far, but 12 regiments could not be expected to hold the gap open without help. Upton needed reinforcements.

Support was to have come from Brigadier General Gershom Mott's division of Hancock's II Corps. Mott's troops had been formed on high ground to the left and rear of Upton's line of attack. Their orders were to advance across a glade, 400 yards deep, and then pour through the hole created by Upton's attack. But Mott's troops came under heavy fire from 22 Confederate cannon almost as soon as they emerged from cover into the glade. Some of the troops fled immediately; others made it about halfway to their objective and then withdrew.

Now Upton had no choice but to fight his way rearward. Darkness helped his retreat. All 12 regiments made it back to their lines, taking with them 950 Confederate prisoners. The Federals had suffered about 1,000 casualties. The 49th Pennsylvania, last to leave the Confederate works, had lost 246 of 474 men; the regiment's colonel and lieutenant colonel were killed.

The failure of Gershom Mott's division to press on drew heavy criticism — perhaps unfairly. Mott's troops had been badly shot up and demoralized four days before in the Wilderness. Nevertheless, there were cries of outrage. "Mott's men on the left behaved shamefully," Colonel Theodore Lyman, Meade's aide-de-camp, wrote in his journal. "General, I don't *want* Mott's men on my left," Horatio Wright told Meade that night. "They are not a support; I would rather have no troops there." Meade soon acted, reducing the division to brigade status and putting it into another division.

Grant, who promised Upton an immediate promotion to brigadier general, shared the widespread disappointment over Mott's failure: "Upton had gained an important advantage," he later wrote, "but a lack in others of the spirit and dash possessed by him lost it to us." Still, the attack encouraged Grant. Upton had shown that Lee's best and most sophisticated works could be smashed. That night an orderly overheard Grant say to Meade, "A brigade today — we'll try a corps tomorrow."

Lee also perceived the significance of Upton's assault — and feared a repeat performance. Writing to Ewell at 8:15 that night, he urged his veteran corps commander to strengthen the Mule Shoe defenses. "It will be necessary for you to reestablish your whole line tonight. Set the officers to work to collect and refresh their men and have everything ready for the renewal of the conflict at daylight tomorrow." As an afterthought Lee added: "Perhaps General Grant will make a night attack as it was a favorite amusement of his at Vicksburg. See that ammunition is provided and every man supplied."

Grant, retiring for the evening, had not

These field glasses were being carried by Lieutenant Colonel Charles Peirson of the 39th Massachusetts at Spotsylvania on May 10 when a shell fragment slammed into him, crushing a lens on the instrument and sending Peirson out of action for a month. The glasses had been given to Peirson by a friend, Colonel Paul Revere — grandson of the Revolutionary War hero — when that officer was mortally wounded at Gettysburg.

thought of a night attack. He had decided, in fact, that tomorrow would be too soon to launch an assault of the magnitude he had in mind. It would be an attack in Upton's style, to be sure, but on a grand scale, and to undertake it would take time. He would strike Lee the hardest blow yet. With luck it might prove decisive.

Grant's optimism and tenacity were reflected in a report he wrote the next morning. Grant's friend, Congressman Elihu Washburne, was returning to Washington. Grant sent him off with a message for General Halleck. "We have now ended the sixth day of very heavy fighting," Grant wrote, adding sanguinely that "the result up to this time is much in our favor." Then he penned the words that would be emblazoned on the front page of virtually every newspaper in the North: He proposed, he said, to "fight it out on this line if it takes all summer."

Grant's reparations on May 11 for the assault on the Mule Shoe were hampered by a sudden change in the weather. Unseasonable heat gave way to uncomfortable cold, followed by a wet northeaster. "A heavy shower of wind, rain and hail added to our pleasure," a Massachusetts soldier wrote sarcas-

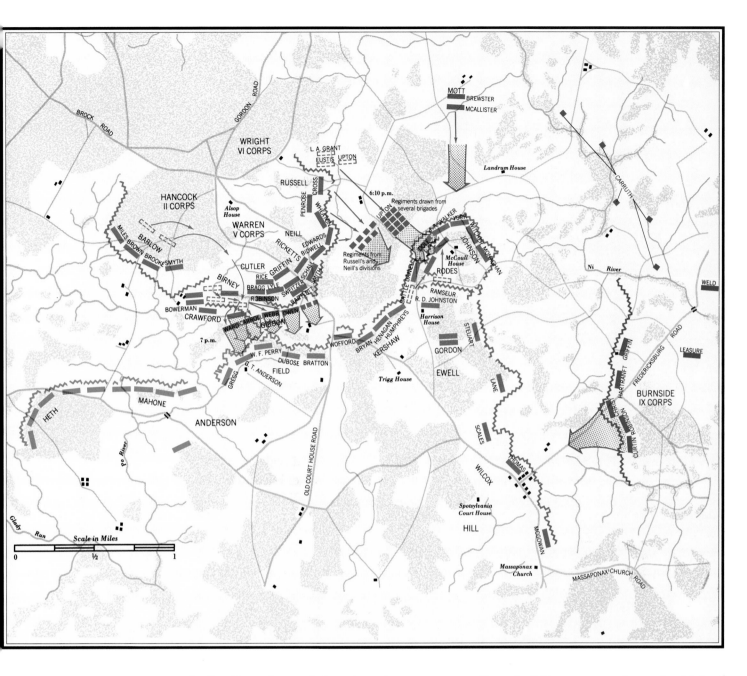

At 4 p.m. on May 10, Warren's V Corps launched an attack on Anderson's Confederates with little success. Two hours later, a brigade of Wright's VI Corps under Colonel Emory Upton spearheaded an attack on the Confederate Mule Shoe salient held by Ewell's troops. Upton's men broke through Ewell's line but were forced to withdraw when Federal reinforcements from II Corps under General Mott were turned back by Confederate artillery.

tically. Grant ignored the rain and wrote orders to Meade. He wanted three divisions of Hancock's II Corps to shift eastward, moving behind the lines held by Warren and Wright to a position directly north of the enemy salient. Hancock, his formations massed for a concentrated blow, would attack the apex of the Mule Shoe at first light on May 12. When Hancock attacked, Burnside's corps, on the left, was to hit the eastern face of the salient. On the Federal right, Warren and Wright were to stand by to exploit Hancock's advantage.

Grant's failure to attack on the 11th of May sparked doubts in the mind of Robert E. Lee, as did some fragmentary intelligence reports. Word had come from Anderson's men on the Confederate left that the Federals were moving east. Reports from observers in a church steeple on the Confederate right had the Federals backing off their line, perhaps moving toward Fredericksburg.

Lee met with Ewell and then called a conference with Major General Henry Heth, the still-ailing A. P. Hill and their staffs. Several of the younger officers present gloated that

Grant was slaughtering the Union army by throwing it against the Confederate earthworks. "Gentlemen," Lee replied calmly, "I think General Grant has managed his affairs remarkably well up to the present time." Then he offered his reckoning — that Grant, blocked at Spotsylvania, would move east in search of another route to Richmond. "My opinion is the enemy are preparing to retreat tonight to Fredericksburg. I wish you to have everything in readiness to pull out at a moment's notice." Lee added: "We must attack these people if they retreat."

The decision shocked some of the officers, who thought the Confederate army's best hope was to remain on the defensive. "General Lee," Hill implored, "let them continue to attack our breastworks; we can stand that very well."

But Lee's mind was set. He feared most being forced back to Richmond and bottled up there. That, he was convinced, would doom the Confederacy. "This army cannot stand a siege," he declared. "We must end this business on the battlefield, not in a fortified place."

The immediate effect of Lee's decision was to imperil the Mule Shoe defenses only hours before the Federal attack was to begin. Many of the guns in the salient were hidden in groves of trees; it would be difficult to deploy them in the darkness to join in the pursuit of a retreating enemy. At Lee's order, Ewell limbered up 22 of his 30 field pieces and moved them a mile and a half to the rear. From there the guns could be trotted out quickly should Grant march east.

The sudden departure of the guns puzzled the men in the Mule Shoe and disturbed several officers — especially when, just before midnight, an ominous rumbling was heard coming from the Union lines. It was "plainly audible in the still, heavy night air," Lieutenant McHenry Howard recorded, "like distant falling water or machinery."

One officer alarmed by the noise was Howard's superior, Brigadier General George H. (Maryland) Steuart, a West Pointer who commanded a brigade in Major General Edward Johnson's division, which held the toe of the Mule Shoe. Steuart concluded that the sound was moving toward the salient. He went to Johnson to urge the return of the guns. Johnson passed the request on to Ewell. The cannon would be back by 2 a.m., Johnson was told. Inexplicably, the request did not reach Brigadier General Armistead Long, Ewell's artillery chief, until 3:30, an hour and a half later than Ewell's promised return of the guns.

In front of the house where Hancock had his headquarters, 15,000 infantrymen had been gathering since midnight for the dawn attack in what a New Jersey soldier described as "a cold, cheerless rain, falling in torrents." Emulating Upton's tactics, the men would advance in a massive formation

Confederate prisoners taken during Upton's charge are herded back to the Federal lines at the double. Most needed little urging to run to the rear — out on the open battlefield, they were highly vulnerable to fire from their own lines.

50 ranks deep, rifles uncapped and bayonets fixed. At 4 a.m. Hancock decided there was not enough light. At 4:30, the men moved out, but even then so thick a fog clung to the ground that Hancock, sitting his horse, could not see the lower bodies of his troops.

The lead division was led by 29-year-old Brigadier General Francis Channing Barlow, a hard-fighting but eccentric officer whose usual battle costume, Theodore Lyman wrote, consisted of "a flannel checked shirt, a threadbare pair of trousers and an old blue kepi." As the advance began, Barlow turned to his staff and said, "Make your peace with God and mount, gentlemen; I have a hot place picked out for some of you today."

Barlow's troops slogged through a muddy stretch of woods, then emerged into a large clearing. They quickly overwhelmed a line of enemy pickets, then rushed toward the spiky abatis. Men with axes were soon chopping paths through the barrier of felled trees and sharpened stakes. Much to the surprise of Barlow and his troops, the Confederate artillery had so far been virtually silent. Scattered fire came from the Confederate trenches beyond the abatis, but nothing more.

Encouraged by the paltry resistance, Barlow's troops broke into a run, the men yelling as they went. All formation dissolved, and the division became a solid mass. Like a great herd of horses, the roaring men stampeded over the Confederate works just east of the Mule Shoe's apex, overrunning Colonel William Witcher's brigade and smashing into the left flank of Steuart's brigade.

On Barlow's right, Major General David Birney's division charged into the trenches held by General Johnson's division, overwhelming Colonel William Monaghan's

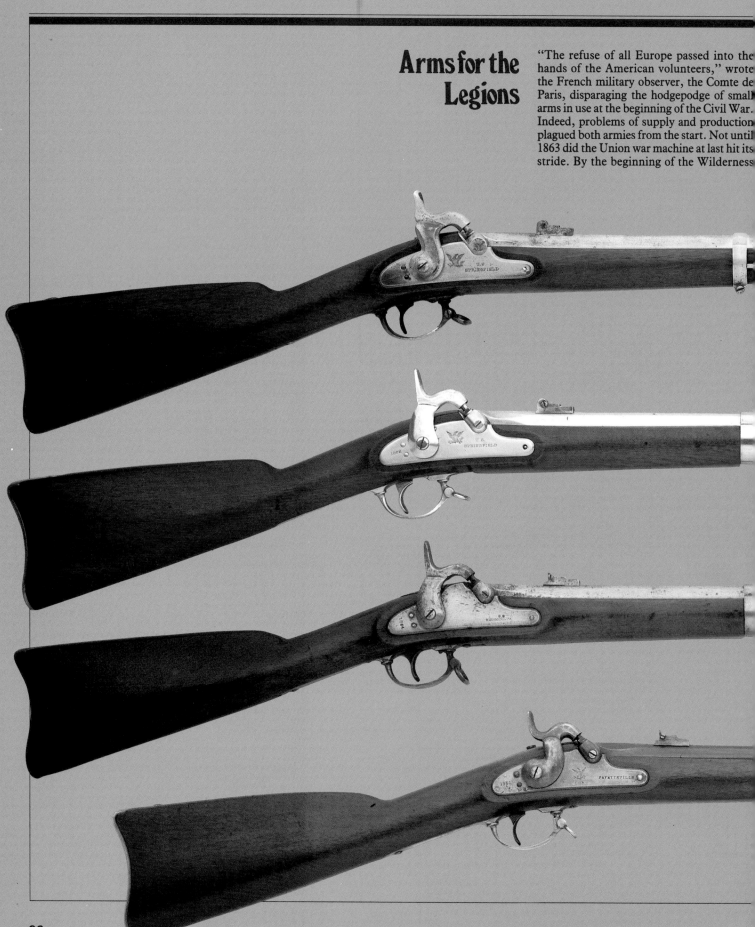

Arms for the Legions

"The refuse of all Europe passed into the hands of the American volunteers," wrote the French military observer, the Comte de Paris, disparaging the hodgepodge of small arms in use at the beginning of the Civil War. Indeed, problems of supply and production plagued both armies from the start. Not until 1863 did the Union war machine at last hit its stride. By the beginning of the Wilderness

Campaign, almost every Union infantryman had been armed with a nine-pound, .58-caliber, muzzle-loading rifle musket. The Confederacy had managed to build, capture, buy and scavenge enough rifle muskets to arm its troops nearly as well as the Federals.

These weapons changed the War. Rifle muskets like those seen below had an effective range of 600 yards. More important, the rifled barrels gave them an astonishing accuracy when compared with the old smoothbores, resulting in well-placed and deadly curtains of fire. As a consequence, the old tactics of linear assault became more costly than ever. New tactics slowly evolved, such as irregular, skirmish-style attacks. Defensively, both sides began to dig in behind stronger and more elaborate earthworks.

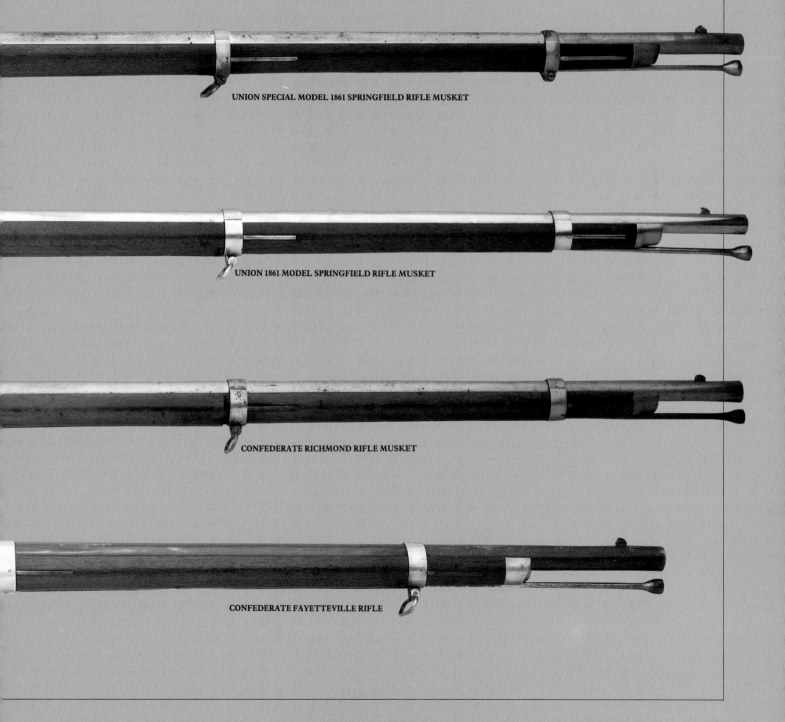

UNION SPECIAL MODEL 1861 SPRINGFIELD RIFLE MUSKET

UNION 1861 MODEL SPRINGFIELD RIFLE MUSKET

CONFEDERATE RICHMOND RIFLE MUSKET

CONFEDERATE FAYETTEVILLE RIFLE

Louisiana brigade and taking Brigadier General James Walker's Stonewall Brigade in flank. "Then ensued one of those hand-to-hand encounters with clubbed rifles, bayonets, swords and pistols, which defies description," wrote Lieutenant Colonel Charles Weygant of the 124th New York. "Officers of the opposing sides cut and slashed with their swords, and fired with their revolvers into the very faces of each other." Then, having broken Johnson's defenses, "the men, without waiting to reform, or for the orders of their officers, rushed on through the forest shouting like mad men, shooting at every fleeing Confederate they saw, picking up prisoners by the score, and sweeping away every living thing from in front of them for fully one-third of a mile."

The crusty General Johnson, stumping around with the aid of a long hickory cane he had used since taking a bullet in the leg two years before, kept hollering "Fire fast! Fire fast!" Recalled Lieutenant J. S. Dole of the 33rd Virginia, "The scene was terrible. The figures of the men seen dimly through the smoke and fog seemed almost gigantic, while the woods were lighted by the flashing of the guns and the sparkling of the musketry."

The artillery was moving up at last, and "Old Clubby," as Johnson was called, exhorted the crews to come at a gallop. Captain William Page Carter had the lead battery, and as it careered into the salient and the first gun was unlimbered, he leaped to help load it. Carter's men got off one round. "Stop firing that gun," a man ordered. Carter turned and found that he was surrounded by Federal troops. Off at a distance, another gun was in place. A gunner cried: "Where shall I point the gun?"

Lieutenant Charles L. Coleman, who had

GEN. GEO. H. STEUART.

Confederate General George Steuart did not bear his capture at Spotsylvania graciously. After refusing to shake General Hancock's hand, Steuart had harsh words for a cavalry major who offered him a horse to ride to the rear. The major then withdrew his offer, forcing Steuart to proceed ignominiously on foot.

been wounded, gasped, "At the Yankees," and then he died.

By this time thousands of Federals had swarmed into the Mule Shoe and completed the rout of General Johnson's brigades. Soon Johnson himself was taken prisoner, though not without difficulty; he was almost shot as he swatted at the Yankees with his cane. Maryland Steuart was also captured, along with 20 Confederate cannon and 3,000 men. Hancock's troops possessed 32 stands of enemy colors and a crucial half mile of terrain in the very center of Lee's line.

Lee had awakened at his customary 3:30 a.m. He was having breakfast by lantern light when he heard the firing around the center of his line. The volume indicated that the Federals were attacking, not retreating. Mounting Traveller, he spurred in the direction of the fight. Soon he encountered his own men streaming past in full flight. "Hold on!" Lee shouted. "Your comrades need your services. Stop, men!" He took off

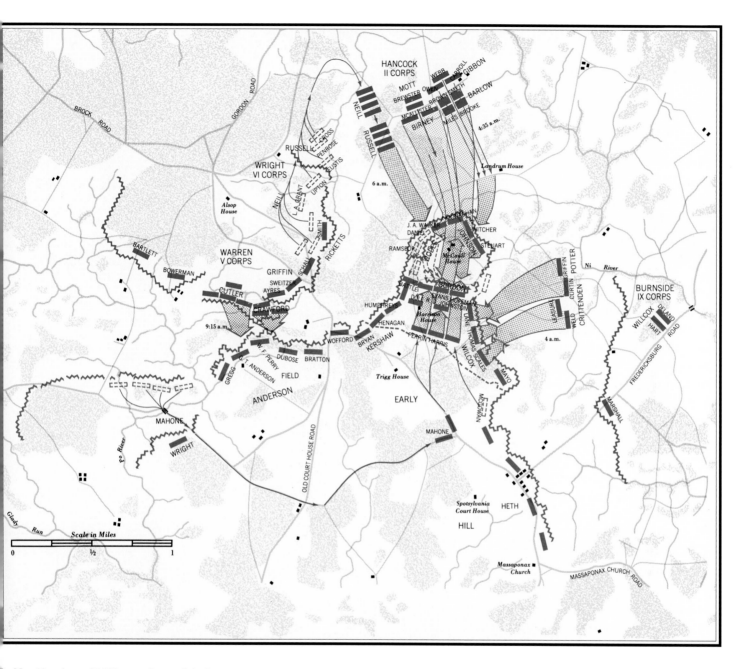

On May 12 at dawn, 20,000 men of Hancock's II Corps attacked the apex of the Mule Shoe and penetrated into the salient. The advance was halted by a Confederate counterattack led by General Gordon, with support from Generals Rodes and Early. Meanwhile, Burnside had hit the eastern face of the salient, and at 6 a.m. Wright joined the attack from the northwest — throwing his men against Rodes's troops in the so-called Bloody Angle.

his hat to make sure that they recognized him. Virginia artillerist Robert Stiles remembered sheepishly, "We passed General Lee on horseback, or he passed us. He had only one or two attendants with him. His face was more serious than I had ever seen it, but showed no trace of excitement or alarm." Stiles recalled that Lee's voice "was deep as the growl of a tempest as he said: 'Shame on you, men; shame on you! Go back to your regiments; go back to your regiments!' "

Ahead of Lee, a second Confederate defensive line was being patched together by

Brigadier General John B. Gordon, commanding Jubal Early's old division. "With that splendid audacity which characterized him," as one of Lee's staff officers put it, Gordon had rushed his three brigades from the west side of the Mule Shoe across the middle of the salient and into the path of the oncoming Federals.

A little later, Lee appeared near the flank of one of Gordon's brigades. Gordon rode over and saluted. "What do you want me to do, General?" Gordon asked. Lee told him to form for a counterattack, as he was doing.

Gordon saluted and started to leave but, looking back, saw that Lee was now riding to the center of the improvised line, hatless, giving every sign that he intended personally to lead the advance. Gordon rode swiftly to his commander. "In a voice which I hoped might reach the ears of my men and command their attention," Gordon remembered, "I called out, 'General Lee, you shall not lead my men in a charge. No man can do that, sir. Another is here for that purpose. These men behind you are Georgians, Virginians and Carolinians. They have never failed you on any field. They will not fail you here. Will you, boys?'"

The men shouted "No, no!" and "General Lee to the rear!" Then, as Gordon recalled, they gathered around Traveller, grabbed the bridle and turned horse and rider back. Lee did not resist and was soon safely behind the fighting front.

At 5:30, Gordon ordered a charge. The line was not wide enough to stretch across the entire salient, but what there was of it — three brigades — went forward as a furious tide. And as Gordon's men started forward, two of General Robert Rodes's Confederate brigades swung into action on Gordon's left. One of them slowed down after its commander, Brigadier General Junius Daniel, was mortally wounded, but Brigadier General Stephen Dodson Ramseur's North Carolinians forged ahead. Three horses were shot under Ramseur in the charge and a bullet ripped through his right arm. Still he led his men forward, seemingly, one man wrote, "an angel of war."

Gordon's desperate assault staggered Hancock's attack — which by now was losing momentum. The men of Brigadier General John Gibbon's Federal division were piling

The toughest fight yet — The fight for the

up as they tried to funnel into the crowded salient. Meanwhile, the Union brigades within the Mule Shoe were dissolving into an unmanageable mob. Commanders were losing control; a soldier in the 17th Maine recalled that "officers were giving orders to a dozen different organizations."

The impact of Gordon's attack pushed the confused Federals back toward the toe of the Mule Shoe; eventually, however, the men of the first Federal waves got back into the trenches they had captured earlier and poured fire into the ranks of the Confederates, managing to stop their counterattack.

While the troops in the apex of the Mule Shoe continued this ugly struggle, fighting broke out on the salient's western face. There, at 6 a.m., several brigades of Wright's VI Corps struck hard at the trenches now held by some of Rodes's troops. As Wright's massed infantry, led by Emory Upton's hard-fighting brigade, moved up a slope toward the Confederates, artillery fire piled up Federal bodies three, four and five deep. Once the Federals reached Rodes's works, near a sharp angle in the Confederate line, a vicious and seemingly interminable hand-to-hand struggle began. The commander of the Vermont Brigade, Brigadier General Lewis A. Grant, recalled that "many were shot and stabbed through crevices and holes between the logs; men mounted the works, and with muskets rapidly handed them, kept up a continuous fire until they were shot down, when others would take their places and continue the deadly work." One Confederate remembered a grisly detail from the fighting: soldiers placing the hands of the nearest corpses in such a position that, when the hands stiffened, they formed convenient cartridge holders.

More brigades of VI Corps crowded up against the embattled earthworks only to be thrown back by Confederate reinforcements. In desperation, Upton called for artillery to blast a hole through the Confederate line. Lieutenant Richard Metcalf galloped up with two Napoleons from Battery C, 5th U.S. Artillery; Metcalf unlimbered and opened fire at point-blank range. Rounds of double-shotted canister slammed into the defenders, splintering muskets and tearing men to pieces. But the Confederates brought all their fire to bear on the exposed artillerists and within minutes all of Metcalf's horses and half of his men went down. Nearby infantrymen helped the surviving gunners drag their Napoleons to the rear, but the limbers were abandoned, their shattered wheels sunk hub-deep in the mud.

Hour after hour the slaughter continued. The rain kept falling. Wounded men suffocated in the mud and drowned in the flooded trenches. Here and there the firing ceased for moments as bodies were flung outside the trenches so the infantrymen could gain a footing to continue firing. The volume of fire was unprecedented in the history of warfare. Pack mules, each carrying 3,000 rounds of ammunition, brought a continuous supply of cartridges to the Federal lines. Large oak trees were chopped down by the hail of lead and came crashing onto the huddled ranks below. Some corpses were hit by so many bullets that they simply fell apart. It was a place of horror, one that would be remembered ever after as the Bloody Angle.

Initially it seemed to Grant that the day was going well. At headquarters, when he got word that large numbers of Confederates were prisoners, Grant, according to Lieuten-

"I shall come out of this fight a live major general or a dead brigadier," declared Abner Perrin of the Confederate II Corps as he rushed to defend the Mule Shoe against the Federal breakthrough on May 12. A short time later Perrin fell dead from his horse while leading a charge, riddled with seven bullets.

ant Colonel Horace Porter, lit up "with the first trace of animation he had shown." Porter heard Grant say, "That's the kind of news I like to hear. I had hoped that a bold dash at daylight would secure a large number of prisoners. Hancock is doing well."

In a short time, the Federal commanders received a couple of high-ranking prisoners. When General Edward Johnson rode up, muddy and bedraggled, Grant shook his hand warmly, commiserated with him on "the sad fortunes of war," then gave him a cigar and a chair at the campfire.

Johnson's subordinate, Maryland Steuart, was taken to Hancock's headquarters. Steuart struck a stiff and arrogant pose. "How are you, Steuart?" Hancock said, offering to shake hands.

"Under the circumstances I decline to take your hand," Steuart replied.

Hancock grew angry. "And under any other circumstances," he retorted, "I should not have offered it."

Lee, meanwhile, was busy urging reinforcements toward his threatened center. In the Bloody Angle, Rodes's badly outnum-

Log-and-earth breastworks at Spotsylvania, like these near the Bloody Angle, were the scene of some of the worst close-range fighting of the War. Wrote Lieutenant Colonel Horace Porter, one of Grant's aides, "Skulls were crushed with clubbed muskets and men stabbed to death with swords and bayonets thrust between the logs in the parapet which separated the combatants."

bered men were holding Wright's troops, but they could not hold them for long. Lee summoned William Mahone's division from Anderson's far left, the Block House Bridge area; then the commanding general, growing impatient, rode behind Anderson's line to meet Mahone's men. He found the lead brigade at a spot where Anderson's trenches were being hammered by Warren's artillery. The falling shells drove Traveller wild; as the horse reared and bucked, a solid shot narrowly missed Lee.

"Go back, General! Go back!" yelled the Mississippians of Mahone's lead brigade. "For God's sake, go back!" Again Lee was exposing himself recklessly to enemy fire.

Lee told the Mississippians, "If you will promise me to drive those people from our works, I will go back." They cheered and set off at double time to join Rodes.

While the fighting raged hand-to-hand in the toe of the Mule Shoe, Burnside's IX Corps to the east had a momentary success. A division under Brigadier General Robert Potter, a courageous New Yorker, drove the Confederates from their line, taking prisoners and two field pieces. But the Confederates were reinforced and struck back ferociously, forcing Potter to retreat.

Next, Burnside committed General Orlando Willcox's division, but it too was driven back by a furious enemy charge. Burnside barely managed to hold his own, containing the Confederate counterattack with close-range artillery fire. He would lose 1,200 men during the day. His main contribution to the battle was to prevent Lee's right from reinforcing the Confederate center.

Far down on the Confederate left, Warren's V Corps had attacked Richard Anderson's line at 9:15 a.m.; but after hours of fighting, Warren's gain was no more than Burnside's. Captain Oliver Wendell Holmes

Jr., a young officer on Wright's staff, had little use for either Warren or Burnside. That day Holmes wrote in his diary: "Burnside who attacked on Hancock's left didn't make much. He is a d — d humbug — Warren, who is a ditto, did about the same."

As evening approached, word filtered back from Confederate commanders in the Mule Shoe that the men could not hold out much longer. They had been fighting since dawn without rest or food. The answer came

The company sergeants and noncommissioned staff of the 15th New Jersey posed for this photograph just weeks before Spotsylvania, where their regiment suffered one of the worst casualty rates — almost 68 percent — of the War. Five of these men including Color Sergeant Samuel Rubadou (*center*), were killed. Two others were wounded; First Sergeant Enos Budd (*standing, second from right*) survived five bullet wounds.

back that Major General Martin Smith, chief engineer for the Army of Northern Virginia, was supervising the construction of a line of works across the base of the salient 800 yards to the rear—the troops would have to hold on until dusk. But when dusk came, the men were told they still could not withdraw; the line was not finished. "Dark came, but no relief," wrote Captain James Caldwell. "The water became a deeper crimson; the corpses grew more numerous."

The men of Federal VI Corps, pinned down in front of the Confederate parapet, were equally desperate. "We had fired three to four hundred rounds of ammunition per man," remembered G. Norton Galloway of the 95th Pennsylvania. "Our lips were encrusted with powder from biting cartridge. Our shoulders and hands were encrusted with mud that had adhered to the butts of our rifles. When darkness came on we dropped from exhaustion."

Sometime after midnight the battlefield at last fell quiet. Far behind the Bloody Angle, a Georgian remembered, a Confederate band began to play "The Dead March" from Handel's *Saul*. "When our band ceased playing, one of the Union bands played 'Nearer My God To Thee.' Then our band began to play 'The Bonnie Blue Flag,' after which the Union band played 'The Star Spangled Banner;' then our band played 'Dixieland,' and the Union band finally struck up 'Home, Sweet Home;' this probably brought tears rolling down many powder-blackened cheeks in both armies."

Just after midnight the new Confederate trenches were ready at last. Unit by unit, Lee's battered defenders retreated, moving so quietly that the Federals, lying on their rifles in the mud, did not hear them depart.

When the morning of May 13 dawned over the salient, the Federal troops awoke to find nothing but corpses in it. In one part of the Bloody Angle measuring no more than 12 by 15 feet they discovered 150 bodies. A Pennsylvanian recalled seeing rifle pits filled with corpses eight to 10 deep. A Maine lad looking for a friend found a corpse so shot up "there was not four inches of space about this person that had not been struck by bullets."

The landscape was macabre. "The trees near the works were stripped of their foliage, and looked as though an army of locusts had passed," wrote Lieutenant Colonel John Schoonover of the 11th New Jersey. "The brush between the lines was cut and torn into shreds, and the fallen bodies of men and horses lay there with the flesh shot and torn from the bones."

The inconclusive battle for the Mule Shoe had ended. In the two days of fighting at Spotsylvania, May 10 and 12, close to 6,000 of Lee's veterans had been killed or wounded; nearly 4,000 men had been captured. Grant's official toll was equally devastating—10,920 killed, wounded or captured.

Before retiring this night Grant telegraphed General Halleck in Washington, putting the best face he could on his failure to break Lee's line. "The enemy," he wired, "are obstinate and seem to have found the last ditch." A week of stalemate would now ensue, with Grant slowly sidling around to the left and Lee countering his every move. A fight of one sort or another would take place every day, but nothing nearly as horrible as the battles for the Mule Shoe and its Bloody Angle would happen around Spotsylvania again.

The Build-up at Belle Plain

For two weeks in mid-May 1864, while the fighting raged around Spotsylvania, Ulysses S. Grant's 100,000-man army depended for supplies on a tiny Potomac River hamlet called Belle Plain.

This sleepy backwater — the closest spot on the Potomac to the battlefront — became the scene of frenetic activity. Wharves were built with astonishing speed to accommodate boats ferrying supplies downriver from the depots at Washington and Alexandria. From Belle Plain, wagon trains hauled cargoes of food, fodder and munitions to Fredericksburg, 13 miles away, and on toward the front, a few miles beyond. Back through Belle Plain flowed the pitiful effluvia of war: wounded men and prisoners by the thousands.

But on May 24 the Belle Plain traffic abruptly ceased. By then Grant had sideslipped around Robert E. Lee's formidable Spotsylvania defenses; the Federal army required new supply bases on waterways farther south. Belle Plain was swiftly abandoned — to sink back into its accustomed somnolent obscurity.

One of the two pontoon-supported piers built at the northern edge of Belle Plain — the tip of the second is visible at left — juts out 360 feet into the Potomac River. The twin docks, known as the upper wharf, were completed between May 10 and May 12 by men of the U.S. Military Railroads Construction Corps.

A fleet of river craft ranging from small barges to paddle-wheelers crowds Belle Plain's lower wharf, at the southern end of the little settlement. The wharf's U shape allowed supply wagons to drive out one pier, load up and drive off the other — and thence to Fredericksburg.

Horses of the 2nd New York and 1st Massachusetts Heavy Artillery stand tethered on Belle Plain's northern neck, having been unloaded at the upper wharf. Downstream, across the Belle Plain cove, lies the southern neck with its tented camp and lower wharf. Artillery, cavalry and infantry reinforcements as well as supplies poured through Belle Plain to Grant's army.

Sibley tents belonging to some of the 3,000 rear-echelon personnel that kept Belle Plain operating — mostly engineers and members of the quartermaster and commissary departments — are clustered on a slope inland from the port facilities. On top of the rise stand earthworks constructed by the Confederates when they controlled the area in 1861 and 1862.

Wagons of the U.S. Sanitary Commission, the civilian charitable agency, rumble out of Belle Plain, carrying hospital supplies to Fredericksburg. That city had become a huge infirmary ministering to the thousands of men wounded in the Wilderness and at Spotsylvania.

Confederate prisoners crowd a ravine behind Belle Plain, waiting for rations from commissary wagons *(background)*. About 7,500 prisoners passed through Belle Pl

...ween May 13 and May 18; they were held in a series of ravines, collectively dubbed the Punch Bowl, before being shipped to prison at Point Lookout, Maryland.

Contest on the North Anna

"This flanking reads well in the newspapers but when one has to tramp day and night it don't go so well."

SECOND LIEUTENANT GERHARD LUHN, 4TH U.S. INFANTRY

4

In temperament, Major General Philip Sheridan had much in common with his volatile superior, George Meade. Both men were pugnacious, fiercely independent and indisposed to accept criticism. Thus on the night of May 8, when Meade accused Sheridan of being derelict in his duty, the army commander received not contrition from his cavalry chief, but a tirade in return.

At issue was the lost race to Spotsylvania. In the confrontation at army headquarters, Meade blasted the cavalry for delaying General Gouverneur K. Warren's advance for several crucial hours the night before, thereby allowing Lee to reach the objective first. Sheridan snarled back at his commander, complaining that Meade had deployed the cavalry divisions the previous night without even consulting him. He was through giving orders, Sheridan said; Meade could command the troopers from now on. Sheridan ended his outburst by asserting that, if headquarters would only get out of his hair, he and his Cavalry Corps would leave straightaway and defeat Jeb Stuart.

Meade stamped off to complain to Grant of Sheridan's insubordination. Grant seemed to pay scant attention until Meade related Sheridan's boast about knocking Jeb Stuart out of action. "Did Sheridan say that?" asked Grant. "Well, he generally knows what he is talking about. Let him start right out and do it."

Meade returned to Sheridan, ordering him to collect his cavalry, ride south, disrupt Lee's supply lines and strike Stuart. Sheridan could then resupply his troopers from General Benjamin Butler's stores south of Richmond and rejoin the Army of the Potomac. The next morning, May 9, Sheridan moved out at the head of a 13-mile-long column of horsemen. To his division commanders, Generals Wesley Merritt, David M. Gregg and James Wilson, he had said imperiously: "I shall expect nothing but success."

"Little Phil," as the men had come to call the bantamweight general, had the world by the tail this bright, hot May morning. He was leading the most powerful cavalry force the Army of the Potomac had ever mustered — 10,000 horsemen in three divisions, backed by 32 guns. And he was relishing the prospect of what he called a "cavalry duel" with his celebrated adversary, Jeb Stuart.

Sheridan first swung his long column to the northwest, skirting the developing hell at Spotsylvania; then he looped around toward the southwest and headed for Richmond. On his orders, the cavalrymen moved slowly, at a sedate walk. With a force so strong, there was no need for speed or deception. Besides, Sheridan wanted to allow Stuart the time to ride past the Federal flank, "urging his horses to the death so as to get in between Richmond and our column." And Sheridan wanted to keep his own horses and men fresh for the fight.

The march led over the Ni, the Po, the Ta and skirted the Mat, four small streams that combined — along with their names —

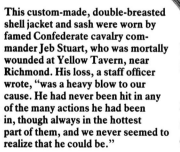

This custom-made, double-breasted shell jacket and sash were worn by famed Confederate cavalry commander Jeb Stuart, who was mortally wounded at Yellow Tavern, near Richmond. His loss, a staff officer wrote, "was a heavy blow to our cause. He had never been hit in any of the many actions he had been in, though always in the hottest part of them, and we never seemed to realize that he could be."

to become one river called the Mattaponi. Soon Sheridan's leading units were at the North Anna River, a sizable waterway a mere three miles from the Federal cavalry's initial target, Beaver Dam Station, a depot on the Virginia Central line. Beaver Dam Station served as the forward supply base for Lee's Army of Northern Virginia; its sheds were full of food brought in from the Carolinas and from the Shenandoah Valley.

Sheridan's troopers missed the opportunity to send these precious supplies up in smoke. The job was done for them by the Confederate depot guards. Alerted to Sheridan's approach, the guards set fire to 915,000 rations of meat and 504,000 rations of bread — enough food to sustain the Army of Northern Virginia for three weeks.

The first Federals to reach Beaver Dam Station, a brigade of Michiganders led by 24-year-old Brigadier General George Armstrong Custer, found that despite the blazing fires there was still plenty on hand to destroy. Custer's men, along with two other brigades of Wesley Merritt's division, managed to burn 100 or so railway cars and two locomotives — 25 percent of the Virginia Central's entire rolling stock at the time. The next morning, May 10, Merritt's troopers tore up 10 miles of track, ripped down tele-

graph wires and, as Sheridan reported, "recaptured 378 of our men, including two colonels, one major and several other officers," all of whom had been taken prisoner during the Battle of the Wilderness. This accomplished, the column formed again and snaked on south, heading toward Ground Squirrel Bridge on the South Anna River.

Jeb Stuart had learned from his pickets of Sheridan's movement almost as soon as the Federal troopers broke camp on the morning of May 9. Stuart had approximately 8,000 men in half a dozen brigades at his disposal. One of these brigades — roughly 1,000 horsemen led by Brigadier General William C. Wickham — swiftly departed to harass Sheridan's rear.

But Stuart had a problem deciding how to deploy the remainder of his cavalry corps. The size of Sheridan's force revealed to Stuart that "Little Phil" had monumental objectives in mind. He was planning either to press on and attack Richmond or to double back and fall on Robert E. Lee's rear at Spotsylvania. To be ready for either maneuver, Stuart would have to divide his command.

He ordered three of his brigades to stay with Lee, leaving himself only three others — about 4,500 troopers in all — to deal with Sheridan's three divisions. Stuart sent Brigadier General Lunsford Lomax and his brigade to join Wickham in nipping at Sheridan's heels, placing the two units under the command of General Fitzhugh Lee. Then Stuart set off on a parallel route southward with a brigade of North Carolinians commanded by Brigadier General James B. Gordon. By nightfall Stuart and Gordon had arrived at Davenport's Bridge, a few miles up the North Anna from Beaver Dam Station —

Major General Jeb Stuart was called "the eyes of the Army" by Robert E. Lee. When Lee learned on May 12, 1864, that Stuart had been mortally wounded, the grief-stricken commander pronounced a simple tribute: "He never brought me a false piece of information."

Waving his ostrich-plumed hat, Jeb Stuart leads his illustrious cavalry up a steep incline in this symbolic painting. In defense of his flamboyant style, Stuart once declared, "We must substitute *esprit* for numbers. Therefore, I strive to inculcate in my men the spirit of the chase."

too late to save the supply depot from destruction. Stuart doubtless watched in mortification as flames illuminated the night sky to the southwest.

But he faced a more pressing problem: to protect Richmond. Early the next morning, May 10, Stuart telegraphed Richmond to alert Braxton Bragg, now Confederate chief of staff and commander of Richmond's defenses, that Sheridan appeared to be moving south from Beaver Dam Station. Reinforcements from the Richmond garrison would be needed, Stuart said, should a fight develop on the city's outskirts.

Stuart then ordered Fitzhugh Lee and his two brigades to circle to the east around Sheridan's column and head toward Richmond with all the speed they could get from their underfed mounts. Gordon's brigade would assume the task of harassing the rear of Sheridan's column. Even though his men were outnumbered better than 2 to 1, Stuart reasoned that he might be able to deal Sheridan a paralyzing blow if Fitzhugh Lee, with support from the Richmond garrison, could block the Federal column from the front while Gordon's brigade attacked the enemy rear.

Having given his orders, Stuart calculated that he had time for a brief visit with his wife, Flora, and their two children, who were staying at a plantation near Beaver Dam Station — thought until the day before to be a safe refuge from marauding Yankees.

As Stuart rode into the plantation yard, Flora rushed out to greet him. He could not linger long enough even to dismount, but he leaned down and kissed her and they talked privately for a few moments. Then he kissed her again and took his leave.

The parting cast a somber spell over the

normally jovial Stuart and, according to Stuart's inspector general, Major Reid Venable, he remained silent for a long time. When at last the cavalry commander did speak, it was on a subject that he seldom mentioned —death. He did not expect to survive the conflict, Stuart said; he did not wish to live in a defeated South.

Pushing on to the southeast, Stuart managed to rejoin Fitzhugh Lee shortly after nightfall near Hanover Junction. There he learned from a courier sent by General Gordon that the Federals were camped about 10 miles away, near Ground Squirrel Bridge on the South Anna. That put Sheridan within 20 miles of Richmond—five miles closer to

the city than Fitzhugh Lee's horsemen. The impatient Stuart wanted to move at once, but Fitzhugh Lee was able to convince him that the troopers had to eat and rest, lest they fall out from exhaustion. The march was to be resumed at 1 a.m.

By dawn the Confederate horsemen had crossed the South Anna, and shortly afterward they picked up the region's main north-south highway, the Telegraph road. Stuart soon received word from Gordon that two of Sheridan's divisions had left Ground Squirrel Bridge and were clattering down the Mountain road toward Richmond. The two cavalry forces were now clearly on a collision course. Less than 10 miles ahead the Tele-

Major Henry W. Granger, the horseman above, was killed by shots through the head and heart as he led the 7th Michigan Cavalry against Stuart's Confederates at Yellow Tavern. Wrote Brigadier General George A. Custer, "He fell as the warrior loves to fall, with his face to the foe." (The man crouching beneath Granger's horse is holding the animal's legs still for the photographer.)

graph and Mountain roads met, merging to form Brook Turnpike, a thoroughfare running straight into the Confederate capital. One-half mile south of the intersection was a ramshackle, paintless former stagecoach inn called Yellow Tavern. By eight in the morning Stuart had reached the abandoned hostelry with Lee's vanguard, well ahead of the approaching Federals.

Hoping that reinforcements were en route from Bragg, Stuart went on the defensive. To block the Federals, he formed a line that stretched across both the Mountain road and the Telegraph road just above the intersection of the two routes. Fitzhugh Lee deployed Wickham's brigade on the right and Lomax's on the left. On a hill near the end of Lomax's line, Captain William Griffin emplaced the guns of his Baltimore Light Artillery.

Around 11 a.m. Colonel Thomas Devin's Union brigade turned south off the Mountain road and thrust hard at Lomax's skimpy gray line on the Confederate left. After a sharp encounter, the Federal attack was driven back by dismounted troopers of the 5th Virginia, led by a fierce fighter, Colonel Henry Clay Pate — who would be killed later in the day.

At 2 p.m., during a lull in the fighting, Stuart received an encouraging message from Richmond. Bragg could field 4,000 defenders, counting convalescents. He had also ordered up three brigades from the Confederate force led by the hero of Bull Run, General P.G.T. Beauregard, who was facing Benjamin Butler's Federal army along the James River east of Richmond. With these forces and Richmond's artillery, Bragg believed he could hold the capital.

The news heartened Stuart, and he chat-ted cheerfully with his staff. He was thinking of mounting a counterattack on Sheridan's flank when Sheridan seized the initiative. First he sent General James Wilson's division sweeping around Wickham's flank, cutting Brook Turnpike and Stuart's natural line of retreat. Then about 4 p.m. Sheridan ordered both Wilson and Merritt to attack the Confederate line.

As Federal horse artillery pounded the Confederate position, George Custer led his 1st Michigan in a thundering charge on Griffin's Maryland battery. Many of the Marylanders had already fallen to the Federal artillery fire. "The rain of shot and shrapnel became terrific," a survivor recalled. "The groans of the wounded and dying, and the shrieks of maimed and disemboweled horses were enough to appall the stoutest heart." Even so, Griffin's gunners took a heavy toll, bowling over horses and riders with double-shotted canister, before being overrun by Custer's Michiganders.

While Custer threw more regiments into the fray, Colonel William Chapman's brigade wheeled into position to strike the Confederate center and General Wilson led forward a line of dismounted troopers that overlapped the Confederate right. First Lomax's and then Wickham's men began to break for the rear.

Stuart determined to recapture the battery and rally the left of his line. He brought up his only reserves — 80 mounted men of the 1st Virginia — and led them at the gallop to his beleaguered left, shouting: "Charge, Virginians, and save those brave Marylanders!" Major Venable, riding at the general's side, urged Stuart to keep out of the fighting. "I don't reckon there is any danger!" Stuart replied, all but laughing.

A Haven for the Wounded

In late May 1864, as the Army of the Potomac moved southeastward in its attempt to flank Lee, Fredericksburg was transformed into a vast hospital for the more than 20,000 Federal and Confederate troops wounded in the Wilderness and at Spotsylvania.

Nearly every store, warehouse and church was used for shelter, and the hills surrounding the town were, according to one observer, "white with tents and wagons." Surgeons operated round the clock. In an 11-hour shift, one doctor dressed the wounds of 703 men.

"Go into the hospitals," a correspondent wrote. "Armless, legless men, wounds of every description. Men on the hard floor, lying in one position all day, unable to stir till the nurse comes to their aid. Hard it is to see them suffer, and not be able to relieve them."

Officers and nurses of the U.S. Sanitary Commission, a civilian relief organization that helped care for the wounded, gather at their supply depot in a Fredericksburg back lot.

A burial detail prepares temporary graves for soldiers who have died of their wounds. The bodies were later reinterred in permanent plots.

Wounded soldiers rest on Marye's Heights outside the city of Fredericksburg. Military bands played lively airs in an effort to cheer them.

The 1st Virginia engaged Custer's horsemen in a swirling melee. A Michigander remembered that "the dull thud of sabers descending upon hapless heads could be heard amid the rattle of carbines and the cracking of pistols." Stuart wheeled his mount to and fro, attempting to rally his troopers. Lomax's dismounted cavalrymen had withdrawn to the shelter of a creek bed, but soon the entreaties of their officers had them moving forward once more. And now it was the Federals' turn to retreat.

Stuart stayed very close to the action. To his resurging troopers, he cried, "Steady, men, steady!" and he emptied his big nine-shot LeMatt revolver at the fleeing Michigan horsemen. Soon the area was cleared of all but disordered clusters of Federals, most of whom had lost their mounts and were trying to get away on foot. One of them — by some accounts it was a 48-year-old private named John A. Huff, a former sharpshooter — saw a red beard, a plume, a silk-lined cape, a large figure on a horse 30 feet away. The Federal aimed, squeezed the trigger and then ran off, his pistol smoking.

Stuart's chin dropped to his chest and his hat fell off. The shock had come on his right side. He clapped a hand over the spot.

"General," shouted one of the troopers nearby, "are you hit?"

"I am afraid I am," he said in a level voice.

Captain G. W. Dorsey of the 1st Virginia helped Stuart off his panicked horse, and several soldiers supported him while Dorsey found a calmer mount. The men escorted Stuart to the rear as the fighting raged around them. Fitzhugh Lee, having ridden the length of the Confederate line to see his wounded superior, arrived in great distress. "Go ahead, Fitz, old fellow," Stuart said to him. "I know you will do what is right."

At length an ambulance was found, and Stuart began an excruciating journey to Richmond. There was no direct route, for by now the Federals held much of the Brook Turnpike. Carrying its bleeding passenger, the springless vehicle bucked and swayed along rutted back roads for six hours, arriving in the city well after dark.

Stuart was taken into the house of his brother-in-law, Dr. Charles Brewer, a physician. Between paroxysms of pain, he asked for his wife, who was on her way from Beaver Dam Station. Stuart also bequeathed some official papers and some of his personal effects, including a pair of favorite mounts — a gray horse to Major Venable, a bay to Major Henry McClellan, another staff officer.

As he continued to dispose of his possessions, Stuart became aware of the rolling sound of artillery fire to the north of Richmond. He asked Henry McClellan for the news. Sheridan had continued to hit Fitzhugh Lee's line for an hour or so after Stuart had been removed from the field, McClellan reported. Lee's line had slowly given way, and the Union general, shouldering aside the Confederates, had continued southward down the Brook Turnpike. By dark Sheridan's cavalry had reached Richmond's outer line of defense. But instead of attacking the capital, Sheridan had suddenly turned his troopers and headed east.

"Little Phil," in fact, had faced a quandary that evening. He was sorely tempted, as he later reported to General Meade, to storm the town. "It is possible that I might have captured the city of Richmond by assault," Sheridan wrote. "I should have been the hero of the hour. I could have gone in and burned and killed right and left." But he knew that he lacked the strength to hold the prize, that in the end his cavalry would be sacrificed "for no permanent advantage."

Sheridan decided instead to withdraw swiftly eastward: Gordon was still threatening his rear, and Fitzhugh Lee was somewhere on his flank. To evade pursuit, the Federals would make for Meadow Bridge on the Chickahominy, cross there, and then ride downstream, with the river between them and any oncoming Confederates. Then Sheridan would recross the river, arriving behind Benjamin Butler's lines on the James River, where he would replenish his troopers' nearly exhausted supplies of food and ammunition.

Sheridan's withdrawal was a risky and difficult maneuver, made worse by a storm so fierce that it toppled a church steeple in Richmond. The rain slowed the long Federal column; the troopers did not reach Meadow Bridge until daylight — and then found that a Confederate detachment had set fire to the highway bridge and the railroad bridge during the night. Fortunately for Sheridan's men, the pelting rain had doused most of the flames — although the highway bridge needed some reflooring. Dismounted troopers from Custer's brigade dashed across the railroad bridge and secured the opposite bank. While repairs were being made on the highway bridge, Braxton Bragg's infantry and Fitzhugh Lee's cavalry caught up with the Federals and joined Gordon's brigade in attacking Sheridan's flanks and rear. A short, hot fight developed. The divisions of Gregg and Wilson staunchly held off the Confederate attackers while the rest of Merritt's brigades joined Custer's in securing and repairing the vital highway span.

Just as they were finishing, General Gordon led a Confederate charge against the hard-fighting Federal rear guard. Gordon was mortally wounded, and his attack faltered. Sheridan managed to get his three divisions across the bridge at last. They made their way without further interference to Haxall's Landing on the James, where they rested for four days and refitted before setting out to rejoin the Army of the Potomac. In all, Sheridan had lost about 625 men killed, wounded or missing, but he had recovered nearly 400 Union prisoners and had captured about 300 Confederates, whom he took with him behind Butler's lines. He could further avow that his raid had damaged the Confederate cause by destroying large quantities of supplies. And what better evidence of a Federal victory could he present than the death of Major General James Ewell Brown Stuart?

As Sheridan's men were moving down the Chickahominy to safety, Stuart was indeed near death. By dusk on May 12 he had been told he would not last the night. "I am resigned if it be God's will," he said. "But I would like to see my wife." A little after 7 o'clock that evening, two clergymen were brought to his bedside. Stuart, always fond of singing, asked them to join him in a rendition of his favorite hymn, "Rock of Ages." The three men sang the old anthem: "Rock of ages, cleft for me, / Let me hide myself in thee." Stuart died at 7:38. Flora Stuart and the children did not arrive until shortly before midnight.

On that same night, at Spotsylvania Court House, when the hellish struggle in the Bloody Angle was at its height, someone delivered a telegram to Robert E. Lee. He opened and read it, then gave a stricken look. Moments passed before he felt he could

speak. "Gentlemen," he said to those around him, "we have very bad news. General Stuart has been mortally wounded." Later that night Lee said, "I can scarcely think of him without weeping."

At Spotsylvania the next morning, May 13, Ulysses S. Grant sent a note to General Meade, still entrenched around the Bloody Angle: "I do not desire a battle brought on with the enemy in their position of yesterday, but want to press as close to them as possible to determine their position and strength. We must get by the right flank of the enemy for the next fight." Grant was trying to find a way out of the murderous impasse at Spotsylvania. "The world has never seen so bloody or so protracted a battle as the one being fought and I hope never will again," he wrote his wife. He would make another attempt to move to his left in the hope of turning Lee's right.

On the night of May 13 Grant pulled Gouverneur K. Warren's V Corps out of the trenches on the Federal right, swinging it behind the entire Union rear to a new posi-

Confederate dead are laid out for burial near the Alsop farm, where the final clash at Spotsylvania took place. Standing by are the men of the 1st Massachusetts Heavy Artillery, who were assigned to help in the grim duty of burying the dead of both sides.

tion east of Spotsylvania Court House. At 3 a.m. Horatio Wright's VI Corps followed, and it took a position on Warren's left. Both corps had orders to attack at dawn after making the shifts of front, but darkness, confusion, weariness and the ankle-deep slime left by rainstorms ate away the time. By first light, only the vanguard of Warren's corps had arrived at its destination. The advantage of surprise was now lost and the attacks were canceled.

"The very heavy rains of the last 48 hours have made it almost impossible to move trains or artillery," an impatient Grant reported to General Halleck in Washington. The roads were "so impassable," he continued, "that little will be done until there is a change of weather."

The weather did change at last, the rain ceasing on May 16. The next day was very hot, and the earth was quickly drying. Meanwhile General Lee, as Grant knew from the interrogation of prisoners, had been shifting some of his units from the left of the Confederate line southward to his right in order to counter the Federal movements. Grant now thought he saw an opportunity at last to break through Lee's infuriating trenches. In strengthening his right, Grant reasoned, Lee must necessarily have weakened his left. An attack there, on the already blood-soaked earthworks north of Spotsylvania, might encounter nothing but a thin gray line.

Wright's tired corps was ordered to countermarch all the way from its new position on the Federal left to its old line on the right. Winfield Scott Hancock's II Corps, now in reserve, was to join in the assault, scheduled for dawn on May 18.

Again, circumstances conspired against the Federals. The attack by Wright and Hancock, planned for first light to catch the Confederate army off guard, was slow in getting started. Hours were lost while the advancing infantry cautiously occupied the original Confederate position at the Bloody Angle, then moved on to the second line of defense the Confederates had constructed in the Mule Shoe on May 12. There the Federals encountered not a thin gray line, but Richard Ewell's stubborn veterans supported by 29 pieces of artillery.

Around 8 a.m. the Confederate gunners could see the Federals in the abandoned works like fish in a barrel and gleefully began shooting. The fight was over by 10 a.m. The Federals had lost approximately 2,000 men. "We found the enemy so strongly entrenched that even Grant thought it useless to knock our heads against a brick wall," Meade commented irascibly in a letter to his wife. "We shall now try to maneuver again," he continued, "so as to draw the enemy out of his stronghold."

Grant possessed no patent on guessing wrong, however. On May 19 Lee, suspecting that Grant had withdrawn Hancock and Wright from their positions following the unsuccessful attack, determined to undertake a reconnaissance in force in the same area. He ordered Ewell to advance his corps through the presumably weakened Union right, cross the Ni and strike out in the direction of Fredericksburg with the objective of cutting the Federals' line of communications and seizing their wagon trains.

What Lee did not know was that Grant's right was not weak; it had just been reinforced by 7,500 fresh men, 6,000 of them pulled from the Heavy Artillery regiments that were defending Washington. These green troops, hastily assembled into a division commanded by Brigadier General Robert O. Tyler, arrived on the field just in time to meet Ewell's attack.

Spearheaded by Brigadier General Stephen Ramseur's brigade, Ewell's troops surged across the fields of the Harris and Alsop farms only to be met by the countercharge of Tyler's Heavy Artillerymen. A vicious battle ensued, the opposing ranks firing volleys into each other at point-blank range. Private Joseph W. Gardner of the 1st Massachusetts Heavy Artillery was overcome by "a feeling of horror at the cries of pain from loved comrades, wounded or dying; the rattle of musketry; the sound of leaden missiles tearing through the trees and the dull thud of bullets that reached their human marks." Suddenly the first line of artillerymen gave way. "With the most terrific yells, on came Ramseur's brigade," Private Gardner recalled, "crashing through us, firing as they came and wounding and killing our men at close range."

As Ramseur's men pushed on for the Fredericksburg Pike, they were caught in a flanking fire and forced to fall back. Ewell committed the remainder of Robert Rodes's division and then brought up Gordon's division, but the Federals had rallied and now were holding their ground. As Ewell galloped across the field, his horse was shot from under him, throwing the one-legged general to the ground and injuring him. With the commander temporarily out of action, the Confederate attack stalled. Tyler's "paper-collar" soldiers were fighting with unexpected gallantry; one regiment, the 1st Maine Heavy Artillery, withstood the assault of Gordon's entire division. By 6 p.m. Federal reinforcements had begun arriving from II and V Corps, and Ewell was forced to re-

Federal troops relax in front of Massaponax Baptist Church on the same day that the church served as Grant and Meade's temporary headquarters. The men in Zouave jackets and sashes are members of the 114th Pennsylvania, on detached duty as headquarters guards.

War Council in a Churchyard

On May 21 the Army of the Potomac shifted from Spotsylvania Court House to new positions near Guiney's Station. Along the route, the commanding generals, Ulysses Grant and George Meade, stopped with their staffs at Massaponax Church, in eastern Spotsylvania County.

On their arrival around noon, Grant ordered the church pews carried out into the yard and grouped in a circle beneath two shade trees. While V Corps supply wagons rum-

bled past, Grant and Meade sat dov with their staff officers to rest, re newspapers and make plans.

By chance, photographer Timot O'Sullivan was present and, with t generals' permission, recorded t scene in a sequence of pictures th begins on the opposite page. Th photographs, which O'Sullivan ca tioned *A Council of War at Mass ponax Church, Virginia*, were sh from the second story, front windo of the church (*above*).

General Grant sits cross-legged, smoking a cigar, in the pew directly beneath the trees. At his left are Assistant Secretary of War Charles Dana and Brigadier General John Rawlins, Grant's chief of staff. General Meade, wearing a hat with downturned brim, sits at the far end of the pew at left, studying a map.

A subsequent photograph in O'Sullivan's sequence shows Grant leaning over Meade's right shoulder to get a look at the map held by Meade, engineering officer Cyrus Comstock and an aide. Seated next to Comstock is Lieutenant Colonel Adam Badeau, Grant's secretary.

aving returned to his seat beside the trees, Grant writes out the only order issued with a Massaponax Church dateline — a dispatch addressed to IX Corps commander, Major General Ambrose Burnside, telling Burnside which route to take to Guiney's Station.

treat, leaving 900 casualties behind him. Tyler's inexperienced artillerymen had lost 1,535 men, but they had bested the Confederate veterans.

With this encounter the fighting around Spotsylvania Court House came to an end. The postbattle inventory proved distressing for the Federals. Grant's Army of the Potomac had suffered 18,399 casualties at Spotsylvania, plus another 17,666 in the Wilderness for a total of 36,065 since May 5. About 4,000 more Federals had been sent back to Washington hospitals to recover from illnesses that had struck them during the campaign. Another 14,000 had either deserted or returned home when their enlistments expired. With Sheridan's cavalry still on its long ride, Grant could count only 56,124 effectives on May 19. Replacements available to fill the gaps in the tattered Federal battle line would not total more than 12,000.

There was worse news awaiting Grant. Major General Franz Sigel, who was supposed to have occupied the Shenandoah Valley, had instead been routed at New Market by a small Confederate force under Major General John Breckinridge. With Sigel in retreat down the valley, Breckinridge was able to spare two of his brigades, or 2,500 men, to reinforce Lee.

The other Federal force on the move in the East — Benjamin Butler's Army of the James — had fared no better. Southeast of Richmond, Butler had advanced so hesitantly that on May 16 Beauregard had seized the opportunity to attack. At the Battle of Drewry's Bluff, Beauregard had inflicted 4,000 casualties and had driven Butler back into a long peninsula formed by a loop in the James River called Bermuda Hundred. The Confederates had then thrown a strong line of earthworks across the peninsula's neck. Butler's army, Grant later said, had been "as completely shut off from further operations directly against Richmond as if it had been in a bottle strongly corked." Since the neck of the bottle was only four miles wide, the cork could be held in place by a small force of infantry backed by artillery, allowing Beauregard to send Lee an entire division of about 6,000 men.

These additions to Lee's command made up for some of the losses — roughly 7,500 men in the Wilderness and 10,000 at Spotsylvania — that the Confederate army had suffered during the first weeks of May. More crippling to the effectiveness of the army had been the toll of commanders: Stuart was dead, Longstreet wounded, Ewell suffering from his injuries, and A. P. Hill sick with some mysterious malady. On May 20, A. P. Hill felt fit enough to resume command of his corps, but his pallor suggested that the decision might be premature.

For all that, Lee's army was a formidable force — especially with the canny Lee in command. He would shortly demonstrate once again his ability to counter his opponent's moves, as well as his sure eye for choosing an impregnable position.

Despite the Federals' terrible losses, Grant gave no thought to abandoning the campaign. Instead he decided that he would return to his plan of sidestepping once again past the Confederates' right flank. This time, perhaps, he would be able to catch Lee napping. Grant sat at his field desk issuing orders for the army to move on south.

First to move would be Hancock. His II Corps would step out in the direction of Milford Station, marching just east of the Rich-

Sergeant William Smith, color-be[...] of the 12th Virginia, took part in [...] fighting along the North Anna [...] spite a painful ankle wound suffe[...] earlier in the Wilderness. It [...] Smith's second wound of the War[...] had been hit in the shoulder and c[...] tured at South Mountain in 1[...] After the War, Smith became a c[...] nel in the U.S. Volunteers. He die[...] a stroke while fighting guerrilla[...] the Philippines in 1[...]

mond, Fredericksburg & Potomac Railroad. The other Federal corps would follow. Since Hancock would have a head start and appear to be on an independent mission, perhaps Lee would be tempted to pitch into II Corps. In that case, Grant would fall upon Lee with his other three corps and defeat the outnumbered Confederates.

Lee would have none of this. As soon as he detected the Federal movement, he dropped back to the south, ignoring Hancock and keeping his army between the Federals and Richmond. He swiftly decided that the nearest position of strength was behind the steeply banked North Anna River. If he entrenched there, he could cover the direct road to the capital as well as protect Hanover Junction, where the Virginia Central Railroad met the Richmond, Fredericksburg & Potomac line. It was at Hanover Junction that Lee's army was to be joined by the two brigades Breckinridge had spared, the division sent by Beauregard and another brigade from Richmond — 8,500 men in all.

There was no need for Lee to hurry. The Confederates closest to the junction — Ewell's corps — had only 25 or so miles to march. Hancock, moving on inferior routes, had 34 miles to cover. Ewell's corps stepped off at midday on May 21, followed in the afternoon by Anderson's men. Lee ordered Hill to hold his corps in position through the night, unless it became clear that the last of the Federals had departed Spotsylvania Court House. At 8 a.m. Lee told his staff, "Come, gentlemen," then mounted Traveller and headed south.

Grant was in the saddle as well. At Guiney's Station, he had his headquarters tents pitched on the lawn of a farm, then rode over to the house to explain his encampment. A woman there told him that this was where Stonewall Jackson had died. Grant said that he had known Jackson at West Point and in Mexico, and that he had appreciated the general's abilities. Further, he said he could "understand fully the admiration your people have for him." The woman described Jackson's final hours and began weeping. Taking his leave, Grant ordered that her house and land go unharmed.

Lee stopped during the night for a two-hour rest beside Polecat Creek, then resumed his ride to the North Anna. He arrived the next morning, May 22, just as Ewell's column reached the river at Chesterfield Bridge and began taking a position from the bridge southward, covering the railroad crossing at Hanover Junction. Anderson came up about noon and moved his two divisions into a line extending upstream about a mile and a half from Ewell's left to Ox Ford. Lee inserted Breckinridge and his two brigades from the Shenandoah, already detraining at Hanover Junction, between Ewell and Anderson. When Hill arrived the next day, his men would extend the line a couple of miles southwestward beyond Ox Ford. It was a strong position, as Lee fully recognized, the North Anna offering obstacles to any Federal maneuver. Just possibly, Lee thought, he might catch Grant's army awkwardly astride the river and deliver a crushing counterblow.

For the time being, Lee wanted to make sure that his troops could rest and recuperate from 17 straight days of fighting and marching. The commanding general, Anderson was informed, "desires that you will place your troops in some good ground on this side of the Anna, where they can get rest and refresh themselves."

Major General Gouverneur K. Warren, who led Federal V Corps across the North Anna at Jericho Mill, was an irascible man with a propensity for foul language. When a Confederate prisoner called him "a good general, but no gentleman," Warren snapped, "If they only think me a good general I don't care to be considered a gentleman."

The Confederate commissary, unfortunately, was not up to the task of providing the refreshment Lee had in mind for his men. "We were allowed one pint of corn meal (not sifted) and one-fourth of a pound of bacon for one day's ration," wrote one hungry Confederate in his diary, adding that since "there was nothing in that country to steal, we were pretty badly off."

Meanwhile, despite their exhaustion, the better-supplied Federal army was in a confident mood. The weather was fine, the roads were dry and the troops were heading south once again. One of Hancock's officers wrote, "There was an idea that we were still advancing, that there was a plan that would be carried out successfully. When we reached the North Anna I think the general feeling was that we should roll on, like a wave, up to the very gates of Richmond."

As they marched into the town of Bowling Green, Hancock's infantrymen found slaves lining the road. The shops were closed and the townspeople were staring at the Federals from porches or from behind shuttered windows. As some of the soldiers broke ranks

Perhaps because of his failing health, Major General Ambrose Powell Hill's performance as a corps commander never matched his brilliant record as head of the Light Division under Stonewall Jackson. The nature of Hill's malady has never been discovered: Speculation includes dysentery, tuberculosis and psychosomatic illness.

to batter open the padlocked doors to the shops, taking sugar, tobacco and other goods, they were mocked by the more daring of the white onlookers. "You'll be coming back over these roads quicker than you are going now!" "Are you going on to Richmond? You'll all lay your bones in the ground before you get sight of it."

The Army of the Potomac reached the North Anna after a two-day march, approaching on a wide front. Hancock held the Federal left on the east, General Burnside and his IX Corps were in the center, and Warren's V Corps and Wright's VI Corps a few miles farther west.

The North Anna, to the eye of General Meade's aide, Colonel Theodore Lyman, was "a pretty stream, running between high banks, so steep that they form almost a ravine, and, for the most part, heavily wooded with oak and tulip trees, very luxuriant." Meade and Grant doubtless failed to share Lyman's appreciation of the stream's natural beauty. Here was Lee, once again strongly entrenched astride the main routes to Richmond, inviting attack. There was nothing

for it, Grant concluded, but to strike Lee's army head on and hope for a decisive battle that would end the bitter campaign.

The first Federal corps to reach the approaches to the North Anna on the afternoon of May 23 was Warren's. Grant wasted no time, sending Warren's vanguard upstream to Jericho Mills with orders to ford the North Anna and feel out Lee's left flank.

Next to come up was Hancock. Grant sent him and his two lead brigades straight ahead for Chesterfield Bridge. There, at 4 p.m., they encountered opposition. Anderson had left part of Colonel John Henagan's South Carolina brigade on the north side of the river behind an earthwork to guard the railroad bridge and the highway bridge. Kershaw's and Field's divisions lined the far bank, supported by batteries of artillery. Hancock swiftly ordered his own guns into action, and for two hours a fierce artillery duel raged. By 6 p.m. the Federal batteries had gained the upper hand, and Hancock ordered General David Birney to deploy two brigades for a charge up a broad, easy slope toward Henagan's defenses. Amid much noise and smoke — and a pelting rainstorm — Birney's brigades rolled over Henagan's position, driving the Confederates, as Hancock later wrote, "pell-mell across the stream with considerable loss to them." Federal casualties totaled fewer than 200 men.

On the Federal right, Warren's corps got across the river at Jericho Ford without any opposition. But then his men ran into trouble. A. P. Hill, holding the Confederate left, learned that the Federals were on his side of the North Anna, advancing through the woods in unknown strength. At 4:30 p.m. Hill sent Major General Cadmus Wilcox's division driving at the Federals, with Henry

Heth's division following. Wilcox struck Warren's right flank, where Brigadier General Lysander Cutler's division was in the process of deploying. Almost immediately, Cutler's division — which included the famed Iron Brigade and the Pennsylvania Bucktails — gave way in panic and joined in a mad stampede for the river.

Wilcox lacked the strength, however, to complete the Federal rout, and the still-ailing Hill did not hurry Heth's division forward fast enough for it to help out. Warren's other two divisions stood firm, and Artillery Colonel Charles Wainwright brought forward three batteries that raked the charging Confederates with double-shotted canister. Wilcox's attack stalled, and his men retreated into the dense woods. Across the battlefield, Warren's troops dug in on the south side of the river.

The next morning, May 24, the Federal situation appeared promising at first glance.

Smoke rises from the twisted wreckage of the Richmond, Fredericksburg & Potomac Railroad bridge over the North Anna River on May 25, 1864. Retreating Confederates had already destroyed the bridge's south end on May 23. When the Federals, in turn, withdrew from the river, engineers from Hancock's II Corps completed the demolition.

In the night the Confederates had fallen back from the Chesterfield Bridge, and Hancock was able to cross the river virtually unopposed. Wright, following Warren, had crossed unimpeded farther upstream. Word had come from Sheridan that the cavalry would shortly rejoin the Army of the Potomac after 15 days of raiding. Overlooked for the moment, however, was the key to Lee's defense: Ox Ford.

Here, for a half-mile stretch, the south bank of the North Anna was higher than the bank on the opposite side. On this high ground Lee had positioned half of Anderson's corps and provided it with strong artillery support. Anderson's men and the batteries could pour a murderous fire down on any Federal troops foolish enough to try to wade the stream around Ox Ford. General Burnside, whose IX Corps covered the ford, reported the situation to Grant and made no attempt to attack.

The rest of the position Lee had chosen appeared on closer examination to be hardly less formidable. The other half of Anderson's corps, along with Ewell's, held the high ground near Ox Ford, facing the Federal center. On the left, A. P. Hill's corps was deployed along a line that ran southwest between Ox Ford and the Little River. The Confederates could fight from a compact, five-mile-long position that described a *V*, the strongest point its apex, Ox Ford. Anchored on an unassailable center, the wings on the right and left could easily reinforce each other, shifting troops to buttress any spot that came under attack.

Grant's position, on the other hand, was decidedly awkward. To reinforce his left with his right, or vice versa, he would have to draw troops back across the North Anna,

march them past the rear of Burnside's corps at Ox Ford and then have them cross the river again. "Grant found himself in what may be called a military dilemma," Confederate General Evander Law later wrote. "He had cut his army in two by running it upon the point of a wedge. He could not break the point, which rested upon the river, and the attempt to force it out of place by striking on its sides must of necessity be made without much concert of action between the two wings of his army, neither of which could reinforce the other without crossing the river twice."

The Confederate battle line was perfect, but its architect was ill. Lee had been stricken by a severe case of diarrhea. "General Lee's indisposition, about this time, was really serious," artilleryman Robert Stiles wrote. "Some of us will never forget how shocked and alarmed we were at seeing him in an ambulance."

During an illness, the courtly commander was never himself, according to his staff; only when he was sick would Lee allow his temper to get out of hand, and now was one of those times. He borrowed a carriage on the morning of the 24th and paid a visit to A. P. Hill. Lee knew that Hill had timidly sent only one division charging into Warren's path the day before, and he sharply spoke his mind. "Why did you not do as Jackson would have done — thrown your whole force upon these people and driven them back?" Hill accepted the rebuke and made no reply. Lee then left him and his corps to carry on with their digging.

As Lee's condition worsened, he became increasingly impatient to attack. "We must strike them a blow — we must never let them pass us again — we must strike them a blow," the ailing leader said. But his own health would not permit him to direct an assault personally, and when he considered his staff he found no one else who could handle it. Ewell was showing signs of physical collapse. Hill had demonstrated that he, too, was not up to prosecuting a vigorous attack. And Anderson was spanking new to corps command. "We must destroy this Army of Grant's before he gets to the James River," Lee told Jubal Early, who would soon assume command for the ailing Ewell. "If he gets there it will become a siege, and then it will be a mere question of time."

A pair of Grant's officers, meanwhile, decided to probe Lee's defenses to see just what sort of odds the Federal army faced. One of them was Hancock, who wanted to find out how many Confederates lay between his bridgehead and Hanover Junction to the south. At 3 p.m. on May 24 he ordered one of Brigadier General John Gibbon's brigades to test the Confederate position. The brigade, led by Colonel Thomas Smyth, collided with entrenched troops from Ewell's and Anderson's corps. The combative Smyth soon called for reinforcements. In short order, Gibbon's entire division was locked in furious combat near the Doswell family plantation. By late afternoon Gibbon had succeeded in capturing a section of Ewell's line that lay inside a thick patch of woods. But then Brigadier General Bryan Grimes's Confederate brigade launched a counterattack that halted the Federal breakthrough and regained much of the lost ground at bayonet point. A heavy rain began to fall, but it was almost midnight before the inconclusive fighting ended.

On the Federal right another — and wholly unauthorized — attack was launched the

same afternoon by one of IX Corps's brigades. This assault was headed by a brigadier general from New York named James H. Ledlie, who was obviously intoxicated at the time. "The general was inspired with that artificial courage known throughout the army as 'Dutch courage,' " recalled Captain John Anderson of the 57th Massachusetts, which lost heavily during the fracas. Dreaming of martial glory — and disobeying the orders of his division commander, General Thomas L. Crittenden, to remain on the defensive — Ledlie pushed his way across the North Anna near Ox Ford and ordered his troops to attack a virtually impregnable part of A. P. Hill's line.

After charging through a hail of musketry, Ledlie's men had almost reached the Confederate earthworks when, Captain An-

The men of Company B, 170th New York Volunteers, play cards, read and smoke as they relax in an open field at the beginning of General Grant's campaign. About three weeks later, in the fighting near Chesterfield Bridge on the North Anna, the 170th, a regiment of Irish-Americans, suffered 22 killed, 55 wounded and 22 missing — one of the highest regimental casualty rates in the battle.

derson remembered, "suddenly every gun flashed out a shower of grape and canister which shook the very ground and swept everything in front. Beneath the clouds of rising smoke the Confederate infantry could be seen rapidly advancing and closing in from the right and left. The gallant charge went no farther, but turned into a complete rout." The Federals broke and ran for the river with General Nathaniel Harris' Mississippi brigade at their heels. General Ledlie, raving with what one soldier euphemistically termed "sunstroke," made no attempt to rally his men; instead he retreated to the banks of the North Anna as swiftly as the most panic-stricken of his soldiers.

The entire affair would have been ludicrous except for the fact that there were 220 soldiers killed, wounded or missing—and that Ledlie's superiors unaccountably failed to punish him or to relieve him of command. He and his "Dutch courage" would help botch a far more important attack two months later at Petersburg.

Thanks in part to Ledlie's unauthorized attack, Federal casualties on the North Anna stood at 1,973, more than twice those suffered by the Confederates. Having seen two assaults so strongly opposed, Grant concluded that a concentrated push would be folly. In a wire to General Halleck, Grant reported: "To make an attack from either wing would cause a slaughter of our men that even success would not justify." Therefore, Grant proposed that he would withdraw on the night of the 26th and proceed to sidle once again around Lee's right.

Despite the standoff, Grant felt there was ample reason for optimism. The fire, he believed, was fading from the Army of Northern Virginia. Given such strong works, why had Lee not attacked him? "Lee's army is really whipped," he reported to Halleck. "The prisoners we now take show it, and the action of his army shows it unmistakably. A battle with them outside of intrenchments cannot be had. Our men feel that they have gained the *morale* over the enemy, and attack him with confidence. I may be mistaken, but I feel that our success over Lee's army is already assured."

Charles A. Dana, then Assistant Secretary of War and traveling with Grant, was even more enthusiastic than his Union commander. "Rely upon it," he said in a dispatch to the War Department on May 26, "the end is near as well as sure." Dana could not have been more wrong.

Respite on a Riverbank

For four days in May 1864, the armies of Lee and Grant skirmished and sparred along the banks of the North Anna River, 25 miles north of Richmond. An epic confrontation seemed imminent. Tension gripped the soldiers on both sides. Already that month they had endured the ordeals of the Wilderness and Spotsylvania, and had seen their comrades fall by the thousands. "How we feared," said a Union private, "that Grant would keep sending us to the slaughter."

By the third day, both privates and generals knew there would be no blood bath on the North Anna. The Union's bridges led to a dead end; south of the river Grant's soldiers were confronted by a wall of Confederate fortifications.

Confident that their commander would bypass Lee's impregnable position, the Union troops relaxed for a time. With those soldiers was photographer Timothy O'Sullivan, who earlier in the War had often been close to the action. Now O'Sullivan had the opportunity to capture the placid beauty of the North Anna and the soldiers at ease in the middle of a hot, tough campaign. His photographs appear on these pages.

Wielding picks and spades, men of the 50th New York Engineers cut a road along the steep south bank of the North Anna at Jericho Mill, one of two major crossing points. O'Sullivan, a New Yorker, recorded most of the work done by this busy battalion from his home state.

Union guards lounge at the south end
of the Chesterfield Bridge on May
25. Two days earlier, troops from
General Hancock's II Corps stormed
the Confederate redoubt (*left rear*),
silencing its six guns. The attackers lost 150 dead and wounded, but
gained control of the bridge.

The rain-swollen North Anna surges
over a dam at Quarles' Mill, where
General Thomas L. Crittenden's
Federal division crossed on May 24.
Crittenden's men, lacking pontoons,
waded through waist-deep currents
and clambered up slippery slopes to
gain a foothold on the south bank.

Floating placidly on the North Anna,
these two pontoon bridges were built
as substitutes for a railroad bridge
burned by retreating Confederates.
Three brigades from II Corps crossed
these spans on May 24, then retraced
their steps two days later after finding
the way blocked by Lee's defenses.

Federal troops man trenches protecting a captured redan on the river's north bank. Heavy rains on the 25th made the men miserable; water was knee-deep in the trenches despite the shelter of pup tents.

A 160-foot pontoon bridge spans the
North Anna at Jericho Mill, where an
attack by General A. P. Hill's Confederates surprised troops of V Corps
on May 23. Panicking Federals
rushed across to the safety of the
north bank *(background);* Union reinforcements, crossing the opposite
way, had to force a passage by driving
their fleeing comrades into the river.

With the ruins of a railroad bridge in
the background, Federal soldiers take
a refreshing swim in the North Anna.
For many of the men, the lull in the
fighting provided the first opportunity
to bathe in several weeks.

A corduroy bridge of logs and boards spans the North Anna at Quarles' Mill. Working feverishly despite continuous Confederate shelling, Federal engineers threw seven bridges across the river, maintained them against rushing currents and then rapidly dismantled several of them on May 27 for transport to the next battle site.

Appearing relaxed and confident, Federal troops pose on a pontoon bridge. The 1,973 Union casualties on the North Anna were concentrated among a handful of divisions; most of General Grant's battle-weary veterans saw no action.

To Die at Cold Harbor

Grant had his infantry columns on the move down the north bank of the North Anna before first light on May 27. He planned to swing wide to the southeast, keeping the North Anna and a confluent river, the Pamunkey, between him and Lee's army. When he reached the nearly abandoned port of Hanovertown on the Pamunkey, Grant would cross that river and hook to the southwest. Thus he hoped finally to turn Lee's right flank and put the Army of the Potomac between the Confederates and Richmond.

Hanovertown was only 15 miles from Richmond. Moreover, said Grant in a telegram to Halleck, a crossing there "leaves us still where we can draw supplies." Grant's great, slow supply train was vulnerable to attack and an impediment to the movement of the army. To shorten the distance his wagons had to travel, he had moved his supply base after Spotsylvania from Belle Plain, on the lower Potomac, to Port Royal, on the Rappahannock. Then, on the day he gave up his North Anna thrust, he ordered supplies transferred to the small river port known as White House Landing, 15 or so miles down the Pamunkey from Hanovertown.

As the Army of the Potomac marched in two columns over narrow, dusty roads, Lee too was on the move. Finding the enemy absent on his front on the morning of May 27, he marched the Army of Northern Virginia 18 miles south to Atlee's Station on the Virginia Central, along the chord of the arc that Grant's troops were inscribing. With only 18

miles to cover — compared with the 40 miles that lay ahead of Grant — Lee had his lead units at Atlee's Station by the afternoon of the 27th. As the rest of his three corps came up, he skillfully deployed them east of the station so that they blocked all approaches to Richmond from the Pamunkey.

Lee was still racked with the intestinal disorder that was the scourge of his army, and on this day, May 27, Richard Ewell succumbed to the same ailment. Lee had been concerned about Ewell's health for some time, largely because the one-legged general would not allow himself enough rest. Now prostrate, Ewell was offered indefinite leave, which he declined. Nonetheless, Lee made him yield his command to Jubal Early. This meant that all three army corps had changed commanders since the start of the campaign, although A. P. Hill had regained his command. Three of the army's nine infantry divisions also had new leaders, as did 14 of the 35 original brigades. These changes would prove telling in the battle to come.

On May 28, preceded by Philip Sheridan's cavalry, the four corps of the Army of the Potomac crossed the muddy Pamunkey on pontoon bridges. Gouverneur Warren and Ambrose Burnside made the crossing at Hanovertown, Horatio Wright and Winfield Scott Hancock four miles upstream.

On May 28, even as the Federal infantry was crossing the Pamunkey, Lee sent Wade Hampton riding east with two cavalry bri-

gades on a reconnaissance. With them went about 800 newly arrived, green South Carolina troopers. At a crossroads called Haw's Shop, about three miles west of the Pamunkey, the Confederate force ran into Sheridan's 2nd Division under General David Gregg, who was trying to locate the main body of Lee's army.

In the next seven hours the inexperienced South Carolinians became veterans. Jeered at first by Hampton's old hands, they battled with notable courage and tenacity in woods so dense the whole command had to fight dismounted. For a time it seemed as though the Confederate cavalry would win the day. In the end, however, Gregg was saved by the timely arrival of General Custer's Michigan brigade. The Federals launched a sweeping counterattack and, with Custer's men using their rapid-firing Spencer carbines to advantage, drove the Confederates from the field. Noting that he had suffered 256 casualties, General Gregg paid tribute to the Confederate horsemen "who resisted with courage and desperation unsurpassed." The fight, he added later, "has always been regarded by the Second Division as one of its severest." Among the dead was Private John Huff of the 5th Michigan Cavalry — the man credited with killing Jeb Stuart.

The cavalry battle — the largest since Brandy Station in 1863 — did not halt the approach of Grant's four infantry corps. Fanning out south and west, they arrived around dusk on May 29 at a sluggish, marsh-fringed watercourse called Totopotomoy Creek. Lee was on the opposite bank with his three corps drawn up in line of battle.

As Lee saw it, the situation was critical. His army had been unable to make up even half the losses it had suffered since May 4. Moreover, Lee's veterans were weak both from sickness and from hunger as severe as any they had endured. By the time the Confederates reached the Totopotomoy area, some men had gone without rations for two days. Their fast was broken by three biscuits and a slice of bacon. Two days later, they got another biscuit. One artillery gunner who had a biscuit shot out of his hand while another bullet creased his skull remarked wryly: "That shows how foolish it is to save anything." A Virginia artilleryman, George Cary Eggleston, remembered the "unimaginable, all-pervading pain" of hunger as "a great despairing cry of a wasting body — a cry of flesh and blood, marrow, nerves, bones, and faculties for strength with which to exist and to endure existence."

Now there was evidence that Grant was extending his left on a front that Lee could not cover without leaving vulnerable spots in his already-weakened line. For the time being, all Lee could do was try to check the Federal march around his right. The best way to do that, Lee decided, was to strike Grant's left hard enough to halt it. The task fell to Jubal Early, who was holding the right flank of the Confederate position.

At midday on May 30, Early attacked near Bethesda Church with Robert Rodes's division in a headlong charge that swept aside a line of Federal skirmishers and stampeded a part of Brigadier General Samuel Crawford's division of Warren's V Corps. But Early neglected to bring up his reserve divisions swiftly enough, and Warren was able to beat off the Confederates handily.

Lee was less disturbed by the thwarted attack than he was by news that substantial reinforcements for Grant were debarking downstream on the Pamunkey at White House Landing. These were 16,000 men of General William Smith's XVIII Corps, withdrawn at Grant's request from Benjamin Butler's force at Bermuda Hundred. Federal transports had taken them down the James River and up the York to the Pamunkey.

Lee, forewarned by reports, had already requested that part of Beauregard's army at Bermuda Hundred be transferred to his own command. Beauregard had refused, but Lee then wired directly to Jefferson Davis and

Supply wagons of Warren's V Corps cross a pontoon bridge over the Pamunkey River at Hanovertown, Virginia, on their way to Cold Harbor. In the foreground, soldiers are foraging through the ruins of a house.

got results. Without reinforcements he faced "disaster," Lee had said — he had never been so unequivocal — and before midnight, on May 30, he learned that Major General Robert Hoke's division of 7,000 men would soon be on the way from Bermuda Hundred.

Lee's talk of disaster was prompted by tactical considerations as well as by numerical ones. With the addition of Smith's men, Grant had five corps to Lee's three. He also had the possibility of a clear shot at Richmond. There was no reason why Smith could not move due west from White House Landing to Cold Harbor, three miles southeast of Bethesda Church, where Grant had anchored his left flank. Such a maneuver would extend the Federal left too far south for the Confederate right to check it. Once around Lee's flank, Grant could move on Richmond merely by crossing the Chickahominy River.

When he got word that Hoke was on the way, Lee sent Fitzhugh Lee with his division of cavalry to secure the Cold Harbor crossroads. Fitzhugh Lee's instructions were to hang on by any means until Hoke arrived. Grant recognized the tactical importance of Cold Harbor as well as Lee did, and on May 31 he sent Sheridan and a strong force of cavalry south in the direction of the crossroads to protect the Union army's left flank.

Cold Harbor was little more than a dusty intersection where five roads met. One of the roads went eastward to White House Landing, another northwest to Bethesda Church. These two roads provided vital links, connecting Grant's army with its supply base and offering a way for Grant to extend his left flank. The name of the place seemed to make no sense. There was no harbor, and the temperature these days was running close to 100°. One explanation of the name tied it to an English expression meaning a place that housed the traveler overnight but did not have hot meals. In any event, nothing was there save a tumbledown tavern in a triangular grove of trees — and a crossroads important to both armies.

In the early afternoon of May 31, Fitzhugh Lee heard from his pickets that Sheridan's troopers were coming. When Sheridan rode up with Brigadier General Alfred Torbert's division, he found Fitzhugh Lee's men on the outskirts of Cold Harbor with the crossroads at their backs. Torbert's three brigades under Wesley Merritt, George Custer and Thomas Devin fanned out, attacking down several of the roads leading into Cold Harbor and driving the Confederates back into previously prepared breastworks. Once in their fortified position, however, the Confederates were able to fend off repeated attacks.

It was a hard, slow and costly afternoon, with Fitzhugh Lee wondering where Hoke was, and Sheridan wondering the same about Smith. As it happened, Smith's orders had been to head northwest and come in behind the Federals on Totopotomoy Creek, and Grant or his chief of staff, John Rawlins, unaccountably had failed to change the orders and redirect Smith toward Cold Harbor. By nightfall, Smith had overshot the cavalry action and had left it six miles behind, off his left flank. His corps would not get straightened around and find the action until noon the next day.

Hoke's lead brigade, a little soft from its relative inactivity at Bermuda Hundred, did not reach Cold Harbor until late in the afternoon of May 31. By then the tide was already changing. A portion of Merritt's brigade rolled up the Confederates' left flank while a squadron of Custer's 1st Michigan charged the Confederate works with drawn sabers. Fitzhugh Lee's cavalrymen, abandoning their defenses, were swept out of Cold Harbor, leaving their dead and wounded on the field. Sheridan ordered his troopers forward and took the crossroads.

But then Sheridan was overcome by doubt. With the approach of the rest of Hoke's division, "Little Phil" feared he could not defend Cold Harbor. He sent word to Meade: "I do not feel able to hold this place. With the heavy odds against me here, I do not think it prudent to hold on."

Sheridan had already begun a withdrawal when, as Torbert remembered, a dispatch arrived from General Meade ordering Sheridan to "hold on to all he had gained at Cold Harbor at all hazards; that the Sixth Corps would be up in the morning to relieve the cavalry." Torbert immediately faced about. The Federal cavalry spent the night throwing up temporary breastworks. Meanwhile, Horatio Wright's VI Corps was making a grueling nighttime march from the Federal right, circling behind the army to come to Sheridan's support.

Cold Harbor was in Grant's hands, but Lee was determined to retake it. He would use Hoke's division and Anderson's corps of three divisions, which he ordered over from the Confederate left. Anderson would be in charge of the joint operation.

The orders reached Anderson at 3 p.m. on May 31, and he started pulling out immediately. Before dawn on the hot day of June 1 he had Kershaw's division on Hoke's left and ready to fight. Anderson figured that those two divisions could push back Sheridan's dismounted cavalry, then strike at any approaching Union columns as his other two divisions came into line. Anderson's move-

ment from the Confederate left had been carried out with such dispatch that the nearest Federal foot soldiers — advance elements of Wright's VI Corps — were still four hours away from the Cold Harbor area.

Unfortunately for the Confederates, the lead brigade in Kershaw's division was commanded by an inexperienced colonel named Lawrence Keitt and included a green regiment, the 20th South Carolina. Keitt had arrived with this newly raised unit just a week before. Because of the political power he wielded in his home state — he was a former Congressman and fire-breathing secessionist — Keitt had been given command of a full brigade. Now he rode recklessly into the first battle he had ever seen. He looked "like a knight of old," recalled Captain Augustus Dickert of another South Carolina unit. Mounted on his "superb iron-gray," Dickert wrote, Keitt seemed "the embodiment of the true chevalier."

But this brave cavalier did not last long. As he galloped across an open field, trying to rally the already-faltering men of the 20th South Carolina, Keitt was toppled from his horse, mortally wounded, by the first Federal volley. With that the green South Carolinians ran pell-mell for the rear, forcing veterans on their flanks to give way. The panic spread quickly and soon the entire brigade had halted, with some of the men on the ground trying to burrow into the earth. "I have never seen any body of troops in such a condition of utter demoralization," recalled Robert Stiles of a nearby artillery unit.

Kershaw eventually got his men turned around, but Sheridan had no difficulty hanging onto the crossroads until 10 a.m., when the weary men of Wright's VI Corps began arriving on Sheridan's left to secure the posi-

Confederate Colonel James Terrill, commander of the 13th Virginia in Early's division, was killed in the fighting around Bethesda Church on May 30. Nominated as a brigadier general, Terrill was confirmed in the rank by the Confederate Senate the day after his death. His brother, William, a Union general, had been killed at Perryville, Kentucky, in 1862.

tion for the Union. Wright's men started digging in at once, and the Confederates opposite, now strengthened by the rest of Anderson's corps, did the same.

More Federals soon arrived; Smith's XVIII Corps filed in around noon after its roundabout march from White House Landing. And now that Smith's and Wright's two corps were joined at last at Cold Harbor, Meade proposed an immediate attack. Grant agreed: If nothing else, a push forward might put the Federals in a better position for a breakthrough the next day.

A concentrated assault began at 4:30 p.m., with Smith's troops on the right of the east-west road to Richmond and the VI Corps on the left. The Confederates, working fast, had made an abatis of felled trees and sharpened saplings 30 yards in front of their first line of entrenchments. When the Federals reached the barrier, they were met with a volley so intense that a survivor likened it to "a sheet of flame, sudden as lightning, red as blood, and so near that it seemed to singe the men's faces." It was hell "turned up sideways," said a New York Heavy Artilleryman.

Then up and down the line the Federals recovered and returned the fire. "The whole line thundered with the incessant volleys of musketry," surgeon George T. Stevens of the 77th New York wrote. "Hundreds of our brave fellows were falling on every side." Amid the chaos were feats of valor. In the forefront of Smith's XVIII Corps, Captain W. S. Hubbell of the 21st Connecticut watched as a young Federal brigade commander, Colonel Guy V. Henry, rode at a gallop over the enemy parapet and, standing coolly in the stirrups on his dying horse, emptied his revolver "into the very faces of the awestruck foe."

It was six Union divisions against Anderson's four, and for a moment it looked as though the Federals might push through. At one point a brigade posted on the right of the Confederate line gave way, but even as the Union troops were taking prisoners there, Anderson called up a reserve brigade and rushed it in to plug the gap.

Emory Upton, newly promoted to brigadier general for his brilliant assault on the Confederate works at Spotsylvania, was active on the front line. His horse was shot from under him, but he kept leading his brigade on foot. When an officer said he doubted that his men could stop a counterattack, Upton snapped, "Catch them on your bayonets and pitch them over your heads!"

When night came, the firing sputtered away. The Federals had lost about 2,200 troops and taken 750 prisoners. They had made a few slight gains but paid a high price—not only in casualties but in morale. The Heavy Artillery regiments, which had just come from Washington, were especially hard-hit. Everyone sensed that the fight was not over and that the bloodshed would continue. In fact, Grant was already preparing for another and larger attack on the next day, June 2. That night he told Hancock to take II Corps from its position on the extreme right and march it around the rear of the Union army to bring it up beside Wright's VI Corps on the extreme left. Once in position, Hancock was to join a massive dawn offensive that would be launched by all five Union army corps.

Grant decided to make the main thrust against Lee's right. Anderson's Confederates there had been heavily engaged on June 1, and it seemed unlikely that they had found the time to build substantial defenses. If the attack succeeded, Lee's right would be driven back into the Chickahominy, with no time or space to recover.

The three Union corps on the left — those of Hancock, Wright and Smith — would do most of the fighting. But the two corps to the north of them — Warren's and Burnside's — would not be idle. Acting on reports that Lee was strengthening his right, Grant and Meade reasoned that he must be drawing troops from his left and that he was therefore vulnerable to attack on that flank. Accordingly, Meade ordered Warren and Burnside to hit Lee's left in the morning "at all hazards." If by any chance Lee's left was stronger than Meade thought it was, the enemy's right must be weaker, and the attack there would surely succeed.

Meade was correct in assuming that Lee had been robbing his left and center to bolster his right. Indeed, Lee was shifting the weight of the entire Confederate line to the right flank, sending the divisions of Generals John Breckinridge, William Mahone and Cadmus Wilcox south to fill the gap between Cold Harbor and the Chickahominy. Henry

Heth remained on the extreme left, entrenched behind heavy fortifications and with cavalry patrolling his flank. When the movements and the diggings were done, the seven-mile Confederate front would stretch in a great crescent from the Totopotomoy on its left to the Chickahominy on its right. Anchored on the two watercourses, Lee's position would be nearly impossible to flank.

Seeing the Confederates reinforcing heavily on his front on the night of June 1, Horatio Wright warned Grant that unless an attack were launched at dawn as planned, he risked losing what little he had gained. But the attack did not come at dawn, and the consequences would prove critical.

Hancock's corps, in making the nine-mile march from the right to the left of the Federal line, had encountered unforeseen difficulties. "The night was dark, the heat and dust oppressive, and the roads unknown," as Hancock himself expressed it. Lacking adequate maps, the corps took a wrong turn, marched six miles more than it should have and did not reach its destination until 6:30 a.m. An attack now was out of the question. "We were in a condition of utter physical exhaustion," recalled a soldier of the 4th Ohio. Grant rescheduled the attack for dawn the following day.

Fighting flared up briefly on the afternoon of June 2 — Early's corps, reinforced by Heth's division, hit Burnside and Warren at the north end of the Union line, taking prisoners and driving Union skirmishers back on their works around Bethesda Church. But the attack was quickly contained. In late afternoon, rain began to fall heavily, ending offensive operations for the day. Both armies settled down to wait for the battle they knew was coming the next morning.

Barges and other vessels lie moored along the Pamunkey River at White House Landing, where supplies brought by water from Washington and Alexandria were loaded on wagons and hauled to the Federal troops at Cold Harbor. The landing had been General George McClellan's supply depot two years earlier, during the Seven Days' Battles.

In the Union encampments, the much-feared Confederate earthworks seemed to be on everyone's mind. Meade worried that if Lee's veterans were given much more time "they will dig in so as to prevent any advance on our part." Indeed, the postponement of the Federal attack gave the Confederates 24 precious hours in which to dig, and they used their time well. Along the low ridges they constructed a lacework of trenches, with artillery skillfully placed to lay down a cross fire on every avenue of approach. "Intricate, zig-zagged lines within lines, lines protecting flanks of lines, lines built to enfilade an opposing line, lines within which lies a battery," marveled a newspaper correspondent who later walked over the ground. It was "a maze and labyrinth of works within works," he concluded. Yet the Confederates folded their trenches into the terrain so ingeniously that, from the Union perspective, the defenses did not look nearly so threatening as those at Spotsylvania or on the North Anna.

But in their bones the Federal infantry knew: Whatever the Confederates had been preparing, the Union soldiers would have to pay. There was a sense of foreboding in the air. Unable to sleep, the men read and reread letters from home or, recalled Private William Derby of the 27th Massachusetts, "sat pale and thoughtful, forming resolutions."

In the night, after the rain had turned to hail and then to drizzle, Federal soldiers in the extreme front line began taking off their coats. As Horace Porter, one of Grant's staff officers, passed among them, it seemed to him that the men were sewing their uniforms — an odd chore at a time like this. Looking closer, Porter found that "the men were calmly writing their names and home addresses on slips of paper and pinning them on the backs of their coats, so that their bodies might be recognized and their fate made known to their families at home."

If the men were profoundly uneasy, so were their commanders. The upcoming battle was perceived as critical throughout the Union command: "Every one felt that this was to be the final struggle," recalled Lieutenant Colonel Martin T. McMahon, chief of staff of Wright's VI Corps. "No further wheeling of corps from right to left, no further dusty marches."

Yet Grant had not given specific instructions for the attack. He left it up to the corps commanders to decide where they would hit the Confederate lines and how they would communicate to coordinate their operations. More unsettling, no one from Grant's or Meade's headquarters had reconnoitered the Confederate positions. Meade had simply said, in postponing the attack from June 2 to June 3, that "corps commanders will employ the interim in making examinations of the ground on their front and perfecting the arrangements for the assault."

One corps commander, William Smith, was "aghast at the reception of such an order, which proved conclusively the utter absence of any military plan." He quickly asked General Wright, on his left, to explain his plan of attack so that the two of them — at least — could act in unison. Wright said that he was just "going to pitch in" — thus reinforcing Smith's belief that Wright had no plan at all. The whole attack, said Smith angrily to his staff, was "simply an order to slaughter my best troops."

A little after midnight the Federal soldiers were issued two days' rations — hardtack, coffee and sugar — and by 3:30 a.m. they were forming in line of battle. The early-

These two Confederate officers — First Lieutenant Romulus Cox of the 52nd North Carolina (*above*) and Major Caleb Smith of the 49th Virginia — fought with General Jubal Early along the Shady Grove Church road at Cold Harbor. At the time, both men were recovering from wounds sustained in earlier campaigns.

morning chill and the swampy odors from the river made the mood more dismal, remembered Captain W. S. Hubbell of the 21st Connecticut: "The hopeless look which many of the soldiers wore was quite noticeable. They did not expect to succeed."

The rain stopped just before first light. The Union assault troops looking west from their rifle pits saw an apparently empty and featureless plain stretching away before them to a long line of low, flat hills.

At 4:30 a.m. buglers sounded the advance. Along two miles of line, more than 50,000 infantrymen of II, VI and XVIII Corps began clambering out of their works and moving on the Confederate fortifications, still wreathed in morning mists, several hundred yards away.

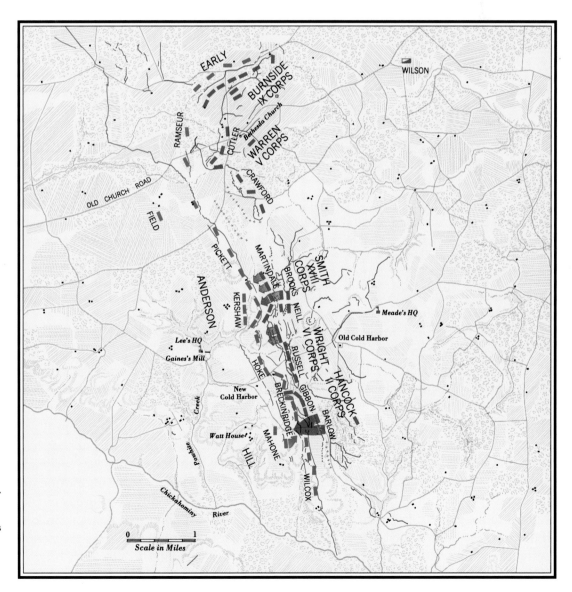

At 4:30 a.m. on June 3, Union II, VI and XVIII Corps advanced on the lines of Hill and Anderson, until heavy fire forced the Federals to the ground within 50 yards of the Confederate works. Barlow's division of II Corps captured an advanced position but was repulsed trying to carry Lee's main works. By the end of the day, the opposing lines had stabilized within 100 yards of each other, at a staggering cost to the Union army.

A Confederate in one of Kershaw's trenches in Lee's center remembered the Union attackers coming closer and closer, bayonets fixed. "Our officers had great difficulty in restraining the men from opening fire too soon," he recalled. "But when close enough, the word 'fire' was given, and the men behind the works raised deliberately, resting their guns upon the works, and fired volley after volley into the rushing but disorganized ranks of the enemy. The first line reeled and attempted to fly the field, but were met by the next column, which halted the retreating troops with the bayonet, butts of guns, and officers' sword, until the greater number were turned to the second assault. All this while our sharpshooters and men behind our works were pouring a galling fire into the tangled mass of advancing and retreating troops."

The Federals who survived those terrible moments were hard pressed to tell what had happened. "To give a description of this terrible charge is simply impossible," Captain Asa Bartlett of the 12th New Hampshire wrote, "and few who were in the ranks of the 12th will ever feel like attempting it. That dreadful storm of lead and iron seemed more like a volcanic blast then a battle."

The Federals were falling, said a Confederate sergeant, "like rows of blocks or bricks pushed over by striking against one another." One infantryman rushing forward on the right of his company looked left and found that he was the only one still on his feet. Another saw all his comrades hit the ground as if on command; when he, too, dropped to the ground, he found they were all dead or wounded. The bravery of one regiment, recalled Colonel Martin Mc-Mahon, was starkly evident in the aftermath of the battle: The dead lay before the defensive work in a triangle with the regiment's colonel at the apex, face down, head toward the Confederate fortifications.

Fighting from behind their breastworks, the Confederates were by turns appalled and elated. "It seemed almost like murder to fire upon you," a Southern officer would later say to a New Hampshire soldier during a truce to bury the dead. Yet when General Evander Law went to the trenches, he found "the men in fine spirits, laughing and talking as they fired." He turned and was shocked by the view to the front: "I had seen the dreadful carnage in front of Marye's hill at Fredericksburg, and on the 'old railroad cut' which Jackson's men held at the Second Manassas; but I had seen nothing to exceed this. It was not war; it was murder."

Under that withering fire, the Federal line seemed to dissolve, so that scores of individual battles were fought in savage and bloody isolation. The fiercest fighting of all was on the extreme left of the Union line, which Hancock's II Corps held: Francis Barlow's division on the left, John Gibbon's on the right and David Birney's in support.

Barlow attacked with the same verve he had displayed at Spotsylvania, galloping forward dressed in his checkered flannel shirt and threadbare trousers. By chance, Barlow's men hit the only weak spot in the Confederate line. This was a stretch of low ground on Breckinridge's front that had been turned into a mire by the driving rain. Here the Confederates had withdrawn most of their men — unwisely as it turned out — leaving only a picket line along a sunken road. Splashing at full tilt across the sloppy ground, Colonel John R. Brooke's brigade routed the picket line and pursued the flee-

The 7th New York Heavy Artillery of General Francis Barlow's division overruns the first line of Lee's works at Cold Harbor on June 3, 1864, seizing prisoners and turning captured guns on the Confederates. After heavy fighting inside the Confederate works, the New Yorkers were pushed back under murderous fire.

ing Confederates. Men of the 7th New York Heavy Artillery, fighting as infantry, battled their way over the nearest parapet, caving in General John Echols' brigade and taking more than 200 prisoners, three cannon and a stand of colors. But Brooke was shot and critically wounded in the attack.

Over on Brooke's left, Colonel Nelson A. Miles's brigade had also breached the main Confederate works. But now the tide turned. The hard-fighting 2nd Maryland rallied, and within minutes it was reinforced by a Florida brigade headed by a tough Irish-born brigadier named Joseph Finegan. At the same time, Confederate artillery on the right and left swept Barlow's Federals with a cross fire—"case-shot and double-shotted canister," recalled a Confederate officer, "fired at very short range, into a mass of men 28 deep, who could neither advance nor retreat, and most of whom could not even discharge their muskets." Federal troops coming up were

stopped by the same terrible fire, with the loss of two colonels — Richard Byrnes, commander of the Irish Brigade, and Orlando H. Morris of the 66th New York.

The noise was infernal — "the fury of the Wilderness musketry with the thunders of the Gettysburg artillery super-added," in the memory of one of Hancock's gunners.

Cut off from their support troops, the survivors of Barlow's two lead brigades fell back from the Confederate works and retreated to a low swelling of the ground, where they began digging in with bayonets and tin cups.

Hancock's second assault division, under Gibbon, was almost as badly battered. Gibbon's veterans moved forward briskly, but with few illusions about what lay ahead. The story was told that after the color-bearer of the 19th Massachusetts was shot down, a corporal named Mike Scannell declined an order to carry the flag, protesting that too many corporals had already lost their lives carrying the colors. His hard-pressed regimental commander offered to make him a sergeant on the spot. "That's business," said Scannell, and picked up the flag.

As it happened, Gibbon's battle-weary veterans fell victim to command carelessness — in this case inadequate prebattle reconnaissance of the terrain. Two hundred yards beyond their own lines they unexpectedly hit a swamp that cut the division in two. As the swamp widened, so did the gap in the division, which was being peppered hard by skirmishers and pounded by artillery. Two brigades at last sloshed out the other side. One of these, under Brigadier General Robert O. Tyler, swept over a Confederate advance position, capturing several hundred prisoners. Tyler was severely wounded in

Soldiers of Hancock's corps work frantically to build log-and-earth breastworks just behind their line of battle during a Confederate counter-attack at Cold Harbor on June 3. The Federals, who had carried no picks or shovels into battle, are digging with bayonets, tin plates, spoons and even their bare hands.

the action. One of his regiments, the 8th New York Heavy Artillery, got within 20 feet of the breastworks but lost 505 men, including the regiment's colonel. "It was horrible," wrote Lieutenant Henry Swain, adding that he found it a "wonder that a single man escaped."

A few men of the nearby 164th New York, an Irish regiment clad in colorful Zouave uniforms, actually got to the main works under the inspired leadership of their colonel, James McMahon. Taking up the regimental flag from a wounded color-bearer, McMahon raced forward and managed to plant it on the parapet before he fell dead. He was hit so many times that his body could be identified after the battle only by the buttons on his sleeve.

Another of Gibbon's brigade commanders, Colonel Henry B. McKeen, fell within yards of the parapet. As McKeen lay dying in great pain, begging his adjutant to shoot him, Colonel Frank A. Haskell took over the brigade, only to be killed himself. The fire against Gibbon's attackers was so intense, recalled a Confederate artilleryman, that at every discharge "heads, arms, legs, guns

were seen flying high in the air. They closed the gaps in their line as fast as we made them, and on they came, their lines swaying like great waves of the sea."

But the Federals could not come on forever. So many of his officers had fallen, noted Gibbon, that the fight was now "simply one of the rank and file." Gibbon's lead brigades wavered and lost formation. Having suffered 1,000 casualties in less than 20 minutes, his division could not sustain the attack. Instead of retreating, the men dropped to the ground, began digging and fired when they could.

The story was the same all along the line. The works proved as nightmarish as any Federal had expected. Because Lee's men had built their works in a zigzag fashion, they could pour a murderous enfilading fire on the lead elements of the Federal columns.

Wright's VI Corps had the reputation of being one of the toughest fighting aggregations in the Army of the Potomac, but at Cold Harbor it was unable to move. The corps attacked with all three of its divisions in line of battle. Both flanks came under long-range artillery fire, and progress was also slowed by thickets and marshy ground. Soon the divisions became separated and the battle line broke apart. One brigade on the right got within 250 yards of the Confederate works, but most of Wright's troops stopped short of the enemy skirmish line. The smoke became so thick that the men were fighting almost blind: One Federal's abiding memory was of "volleys of hurtling death" pouring out from "lines which we could not see." In the face of that overwhelming fire, the attack ground to a halt within 10 minutes, and the men began digging in.

No one along the raging front could see

General Grant (*fifth from left*) stands with staff members including his chief of staff, Brigadier General John A. Rawlins (*seated at far left*).

General Horatio Wright (*center*) poses with his VI Corps staff at Cold Harbor. Moments after the picture was taken, two mortar shells landed nearby.

Photographing the Union's Brass

On June 10, 1864, photographers from Mathew Brady's studio in Washington, D.C., arrived at the Federal camps near Cold Harbor to record the aftermath of the battle. There they discovered that no fewer than 11 Federal generals were headquartered within two and a half miles of one another, and during the lull in the campaign, the brass was available to sit for Brady's cameras.

Brady's men seized the opportunity. The result was a series of images of the generals and their staffs. The four photographs reproduced here show seven of the top officers, including Ulysses S. Grant himself, who had led the Army of the Potomac as it plunged through the killing grounds of northern Virginia in May and early June of 1864.

XVIII Corps's William F. Smith sits with his best commander, General Adelbert Ames, on his left.

Major General Winfield Scott Hancock (*right of tree*) stands in front of the II Corps colors with his staff and three of his division commanders.

much of anything. One of William Smith's soldiers said he never once saw a Confederate, only smoke and flame. Smith's XVIII Corps fought with a desperate courage that earned the respect of the Confederates facing these men. Smith had at least made a reconnaissance, and he knew that marshy ground on his front precluded a major attack from either the extreme left or right of his line. But in the center he found a stream that ran for a distance toward the Confederate lines. The right bank of the stream was high enough to afford partial protection from enfilade fire from the right.

It was here that an attack had the best chance of succeeding, Smith decided. Along the banks of the stream he sent one of his divisions under Brigadier General James H. Martindale. General William Brooks's division and that of Charles Devens were to move up on the left and right to give Martindale flank protection.

As they emerged from the shelter of the stream bed and turned toward the Confederate lines, Martindale's men let out a cry of "Huzzah! Huzzah!" and charged in a column of regiments 10 lines deep. Colonel Griffin Stedman's brigade, led by the 12th New Hampshire, was at the forefront, with Stedman himself urging his men on, waving a ramrod instead of a sword. Immediately the column came under fire so intense that the men instinctively bent forward, as if walking into a gale. The ground reminded William Derby of the 27th Massachusetts of "a boiling cauldron from the incessant pattering of shot which raised the dirt in geysers and spitting sands." The fire, recalled Captain Charles Currier of the 40th Massachusetts, "piled up our men like cordwood."

Carrying the colors of the 164th New York, Colonel James P. McMahon, wounded in the thigh, leads his Zouaves in a charge on the Confederate main works at Cold Harbor on June 3, 1864. Heedless of the Confederates' call to surrender, McMahon clawed his way up a parapet and managed to plant his flag before falling dead, riddled with bullets that sent him rolling back down the slope.

But the men pressed on, the rear ranks stepping over the bodies of the fallen.

Those in the lead got so near the Confederate works that Private George Place of the 12th New Hampshire could see "the flash of their musketry quivering through the bank of smoke like lightning through a cloud." One Confederate officer watched as "line followed line until the space became a mass of writhing humanity, upon which our artillery and musketry played with cruel effect." The attack faltered, another Confederate remembered, and then the Union infantry "began to dodge, lie down and recoil."

Yet even then the attack was not over. Martindale's column re-formed and charged again, this time with the 23rd and 25th Massachusetts of George Stannard's brigade in the lead. Again the Federals were met by an impenetrable wall of fire. As Colonel William C. Oates of the 15th Alabama watched the massacre, he was awed to see "dust fog out of a man's clothing in two or three places at once where as many balls would strike him at the same moment."

Within half an hour Martindale's column was all but destroyed and the survivors hopelessly pinned down. To Martindale's left, Brooks's division had been stopped in its tracks by enfilading fire, while Devens' division on the right had scarcely been able to mount an attack.

By 5:30 a.m. Smith's, Wright's and Hancock's corps were all hugging the earth. Warren's V Corps — stretched out long and thin to the north — did not attack at all that morning, and Burnside's IX Corps did little but capture some advance rifle pits as a diversionary operation. The Union casualties suffered in the assault were appalling: Between 5,600 and 7,000 men had fallen, the great majority in the first quarter hour. There had not been a faster rate of killing, said Colonel Martin McMahon, yet in the War. By comparison the Confederate losses were paltry — fewer than 1,500.

Firing would continue throughout the day, but the issue was decided. It had all happened so quickly that at first neither side understood the truth — the Army of the Potomac had suffered a major defeat. The opening assault had been repulsed almost before the Confederates realized its extent, and many of Lee's soldiers now waited for the day's main action to begin. In fact, many shared the confusion of South Carolina's Brigadier General Johnson Hagood, of Hoke's division, who said flatly he "was not aware at any time of any serious assault having been given."

Lee got the news in bits and pieces. His staff officers began returning from the front about 6 a.m., bearing testimony to unusually heavy Federal losses and a Confederate line that remained intact. The sheer quantity of the dead struck even the most seasoned of the campaigners. "Tell General Lee it is the same all along my front," said A. P. Hill to a messenger, gesturing at the acres of bodies lying beyond his lines. Hoke, too, gave word of the dead and wounded covering the ground and added that he had lost scarcely a man. Colonel Charles Venable spoke for all of them when he said that Cold Harbor was "perhaps the easiest victory ever granted to the Confederate arms by the folly of the Federal commanders."

The sound of the guns had carried to Richmond, nine miles to the west, and late in the morning a delegation of three men, headed by Confederate Postmaster General John H. Reagan, rode out to see what was going on.

165

Lee told them cautiously that his lines were secure so far but that he had not a single regiment in reserve. By the end of the day he was more sanguine: "Our loss today has been small," he wrote to Jefferson Davis, "and our success, under the blessing of God, all that we could expect."

Only slowly did Grant and Meade realize what had happened. Aware that there had been no breakthrough, Meade sent Grant a message about 7 a.m. saying he would "be glad to have your views on the continuance of these attacks." Suspend them when it was obvious they could not succeed, answered Grant, but "when one does succeed push it vigorously, and if necessary pile in troops."

Meade ordered another attack. When he found it impossible to coordinate the broken corps in a joint assault, he sent word to each corps commander to attack on his own. The order was passed down through division, brigade and regimental headquarters, losing credibility at every step. "I will not take my regiment in another such charge if Jesus Christ himself should order it!" shouted Captain Thomas E. Barker, the commander of the 12th New Hampshire. To move the army farther, said another Union officer, "was a simple and absolute impossibility, known to be such by every officer and man of the three corps engaged."

The corps commanders agreed. It was apparent, said Hancock, that the Union assault had "failed long since." He and the two other corps leaders made some token effort to renew the attack, but soon saw it was impossible. When Meade prodded Smith yet again to move forward, he rebelled: "That order," Smith recalled dryly, "I refused to obey."

The men in the line balked as well. When

Confederate prisoners pass the hour in a field at White House Landing, where approximately 1,000 men captured at Cold Harbor were held temporarily. Within a week after the battle, the captives were loaded aboard steamers and shipped to the Union prison camp at Point Lookout, Maryland.

told to get up and charge again, they ignored the order and simply fired faster from wherever they happened to be sprawled. "We were tired of charging earthworks," explained Private John Haley of the 17th Maine. Like many of his comrades, Haley added, he was bitter about "Grant's alleged generalship, which consists of launching men against breastworks."

Finally, around noon, Grant rode out to the three corps headquarters and learned that the attack was a failure. He told Meade to cancel all offensive operations and hold the line. Yet even then he did not fully understand the situation. At 2 p.m. he wired Halleck that the morning's attack had left the Union forces well dug in "close to the enemy." The losses on neither side were severe, Grant added. Meade, too, was still in the dark: He wrote his wife that the battle was a draw "without any decided results."

Either general could have enlightened himself by inspecting the field of battle. Augustus Dickert of Kershaw's brigade recorded that before the Confederate works "men lay in places like hogs in a pen — some side by side, across each other, some two deep, while others with their legs lying across the head and body of their dead comrades. Calls all night long could be heard coming from the wounded and dying, and one could not sleep for the sickening sound 'W-a-t-e-r' ever sounding and echoing in his ears."

The Federals could not get to their wounded. "No man upon all that line could stand erect and live an instant," a Union officer recalled. Neither Grant nor Lee was willing to order a cease-fire that would have allowed burial parties and litter-bearers to go out. The two armies volleyed and cannonaded for three days while the cries of the wounded grew weaker. One wounded man was seen to slit his throat with a pocket knife rather than endure more suffering. Another managed to survive the burning days by sucking dew from the grass. Those who died turned bloated and black, and the stench, said Colonel Oates of the 15th Alabama, became "almost unendurable." It was the Confederates' good luck, Oates added, that the wind was blowing the other way.

By the time the burial parties and medical teams finally went out on June 7, most of the wounded were dead and most of the dead were unrecognizable. There was still some talk, even at this late date, of resuming the offensive, but no one took it seriously. "Everybody felt," said Artillery Colonel Charles Wainwright, "that they had had enough." Francis Barlow, whose division had taken such a mauling on Breckinridge's front, was asked if he thought the works before him could be taken. He replied that his men felt "a great horror and dread of attacking earthworks again."

Throughout the army, criticism of the Cold Harbor offensive was mounting. "The greatest and most inexcusable slaughter of the whole war," said Captain Asa Bartlett, who had gone through it with the 12th New Hampshire. Brigadier General Marsena Patrick deplored what he called "this murderous & foolish system of assaulting." And Emory Upton wrote his sister that he was "disgusted with the generalship displayed; our men have, in many instances, been foolishly and wantonly sacrificed." The management of the assault, said a staff officer of VI Corps, "would have shamed a cadet in his first year at West Point." The cavalry's General James Wilson, who was visiting Grant's headquarters, found the staff wor-

A grisly collection of Union soldiers' skeletal remains sits atop a stretcher on the Cold Harbor battlefield, awaiting shipment to the North for reburial after the War. About 2,500 Union and Confederate soldiers were killed at Cold Harbor; half of them fell in the first few minutes of the battle.

ried that the "smash-'em-up" policy would eventually disincline the troops "to face the enemy at all."

The men needed rest, said General Warren in a passionate outburst to a friend. Warren had just seen a soldier bury a comrade and within half an hour be killed himself. "For thirty days now it has been one funeral procession past me," Warren said, "and it is too much!" Even the Confederates were calling Cold Harbor "Grant's slaughter pen."

Grant was not a man who acknowledged failure easily, but even he felt moved to make an apology of sorts to his staff. "I regret this assault," he said, "more than any one I ever ordered." Thereafter, recalled Horace Porter, Grant said very little about it, turning his attention instead to "consummating his plans for the future."

There was much to ponder. At Cold Harbor Grant lost five men to Lee's one, and his fourth major thrust toward Richmond had been halted. With his way blocked and with no further room for maneuver against Richmond, he decided to withdraw quietly from his entrenchments, swing wide to the southeast and cross the James River to strike at the Confederate rail hub of Petersburg, Virginia, 22 miles south of Richmond. On the night of June 12, his columns began to move.

The Army of the Potomac that marched south toward Petersburg was not the same army that had crossed the Rapidan a month earlier. Grant had lost 50,000 men — a total that represented half the casualties suffered by the Army of the Potomac since the beginning of the War. His officer corps had been cut to pieces, with appalling losses among the regimental commanders. Brigades now were commanded by lieutenant colonels,

regiments by captains, companies by junior lieutenants and sergeants. The troops in the marching columns, one infantryman observed, "seemed to have added twenty years to their age."

Lee, for his part, had gained little save time. Like a skillful boxer fighting a heavier man, Lee had adroitly parried all Grant's direct thrusts at Richmond while preserving his own army from the shattering blow that Grant had hoped to deliver. He had forced Grant to pay an enormous price to reach the ground McClellan had occupied two years earlier at a fraction of the cost. In the process, he had taught Grant, in the words of Meade, "that Lee and the Army of Northern Virginia are not the same as Bragg and the Army of Tennessee."

Although Grant had not made a breakthrough, he had hammered Lee hard, inflicting about 30,000 casualties. And although Grant's own losses would be replaced in a matter of months, the Confederate losses were irreplaceable. Even more important, Lee had been unable to repulse the Army of the Potomac and drive it back to the North, as he had done in the past. For all Lee's tactical successes, Grant kept coming. As he did so, he got closer to Lee's sources of supply, and hence to the means of throttling the Confederacy. Despite his losses at Cold Harbor, Grant still held the strategic advantage. Lee could not move now without exposing Richmond, but Grant could move wherever he pleased, except straight ahead. He had lost the battle but retained the initiative. Hancock might say, sadly and truthfully, that his old II Corps lay "buried between the Rapidan and the James," but Grant was not looking back at old graves. He was moving on.

A Heavy Toll of Commanders

In the succession of battles fought between May 5 and June 12, 1864, the Army of the Potomac suffered 54,929 casualties — 45 percent of all those who began the campaign. The army's officer corps was particularly devastated; leaders whose experience and courage could never be replaced were killed by the hundreds. Hit hardest were the ranks of the regimental commanders, some of whom are pictured here. At Cold Harbor, II Corps lost seven colonels in a matter of minutes. The leadership vacuum created in VI Corps was so great that one officer likened the corps to "an orphaned household." Brigadier General John Gibbon wrote, "The effect of such slaughter on a military organization can be readily imagined. The very best officers fell. When they were gone, the number who served as leaders was fearfully reduced."

LIEUT. COL. CLEVELAND WINSLOW
5th New York
Mortally wounded (Bethesda Church)

COLONEL RICHARD BYRNES
28th Massachusetts
Mortally wounded (Cold Harbor)

COLONEL DAVID T. JENKINS
146th New York
Killed (Wilderness)

COLONEL HENRY B. McKEEN
81st Pennsylvania
Killed (Cold Harbor)

COLONEL ELISHA S. KELLOGG
2nd Connecticut Heavy Artillery
Killed (Cold Harbor)

COLONEL LEWIS O. MORRIS
7th New York Heavy Artillery
Killed (Cold Harbor)

LIEUT. COL. THOMAS BURPEE
21st Connecticut
Mortally wounded (Cold Harbor)

LIEUT. COL. CHARLES TOWNSEND
106th New York
Killed (Cold Harbor)

COLONEL CHARLES E. GRISWOLD
56th Massachusetts
Killed (Wilderness)

COLONEL PETER A. PORTER
8th New York Heavy Artillery
Killed (Cold Harbor)

LIEUT. COL. MILTON OPP
84th Pennsylvania
Killed (Wilderness)

LIEUT. COL. GEORGE DARE
5th Pennsylvania Reserves
Killed (Wilderness)

LIEUT. COL. ALFORD CHAPMAN
57th New York
Killed (Wilderness)

COLONEL ELISHA L. BARNEY
6th Vermont
Mortally wounded (Wilderness)

COLONEL JOHN MCCONHIE
169th New York
Killed (Cold Harbor)

COLONEL FREDERICK F. WEAD
98th New York
Killed (Cold Harbor)

MAJOR HENRY L. ABBOTT
20th Massachusetts
Killed (Wilderness)

COLONEL JAMES P. MCMAHON
164th New York
Killed (Cold Harbor)

COLONEL JEREMIAH C. DRAKE
112th New York
Mortally wounded (Cold Harbor)

COLONEL FRANK A. HASKELL
36th Wisconsin
Killed (Cold Harbor)

LIEUT. COL. HENRY PEARSON
6th New Hampshire
Killed (North Anna)

ACKNOWLEDGMENTS

The editors thank the following individuals and institutions for their valuable assistance in the preparation of this volume:

Connecticut: Stamford — Don Troiani.

Delaware: Newark — Steven Hill.

Maryland: Rockville — Roger D. Hunt.

New York: Hudson — Charles Nichols; Margaret Witham. Rochester — Alice Askins, Rochester Museum and Science Center.

Ohio: Cleveland — Mary Brooks, Western Reserve Historical Society.

Pennsylvania: Carlisle — Richard Sommers, Michael J. Winey, U.S. Army Military History Institute. Harrisburg — Richard A. Sauers, Pennsylvania Capitol Preservation Committee. Philadelphia — Russell Pritchard, MOLLUS War Library and Museum.

Virginia: Fredericksburg — Robert K. Krick, Fredericksburg-Spotsylvania National Military Park. Richmond — Charlene S. Alling, Museum of the Confederacy; Linda Leazer, Virginia Historical Society; Keith Morgan, Sylvester Putnam, Richmond National Battlefield Park; Jenni M. Rodda, Valentine Museum. Woodbridge — Roger D. Sturcke.

Washington, D.C.: Barbara Burger, Deborah Edge and staff, Still Pictures Branch, National Archives; Joanne Cutler, The White House Historical Association; Eveline Nave, Photoduplication Service, Library of Congress.

The index for this book was prepared by Roy Nanovic.

BIBLIOGRAPHY

Books

Adams, Charles Francis, *A Cycle of Adams Letters, 1861-1865.* Vol. 2. Ed. by Worthington Chauncey Ford. Boston: Houghton Mifflin Co., 1920.

Ambrose, Stephen E., *Upton and the Army.* Baton Rouge: Louisiana State University Press, 1964.

Anderson, John, *The Fifty-Seventh Regiment of Massachusetts Volunteers in the War of the Rebellion.* Boston: E. B. Stillings & Co., 1896.

Angle, Paul M., *A Pictorial History of the Civil War Years.* Garden City, N.Y.: Doubleday, 1967.

Bernard, George S., comp. and ed., *War Talks of Confederate Veterans.* Dayton: Morningside Bookshop, 1981.

Blay, John S., *The Civil War: A Pictorial Profile.* New York: Thomas Y. Crowell Co., 1958.

Brainard, Mary Genevie Green, comp., *Campaigns of the One Hundred and Forty-Sixth Regiment New York State Volunteers.* New York: G. P. Putnam's Sons, 1915.

Brown, Philip F., *Reminiscences of the War of 1861-1865.* Privately published, 1912.

Buell, Augustus, *"The Cannoneer."* Washington, D.C.: The National Tribune, 1890.

Carter, Robert Goldthwaite, *Four Brothers in Blue.* Austin: University of Texas Press, 1978.

Catton, Bruce:
Grant Takes Command. Boston: Little, Brown, 1969.
A Stillness at Appomattox. Garden City, N.Y.: Doubleday & Co., 1953.

Chamberlain, Joshua Lawrence, *The Passing of the Armies.* Dayton: Morningside Bookshop, 1981.

Chamberlin, Thomas, *History of the One Hundred and Fiftieth Regiment Pennsylvania Volunteers, Second Regiment, Bucktail Brigade.* Philadelphia: F. McManus Jr. & Co., 1905.

Cleaves, Freeman, *Meade of Gettysburg.* Dayton: Morningside Bookshop, 1980.

Colby, C. B., *Civil War Weapons.* New York: Coward-McCann, 1962.

Commager, Henry Steele, ed., *The Battle of Gettysburg to Appomattox.* Vol. 2 of *The Blue and the Gray.* New York: The Bobbs-Merrill Co., 1973.

Congdon, Don, ed., *Combat: The Civil War.* New York: Delacorte Press, 1967.

Cribben, Henry, *The Military Memoirs of Captain Henry Cribben of the 140th New York Volunteers.* Ed. by J. Clayton Youker. Privately printed, 1911.

Curtis, O. B., *History of the Twenty-Fourth Michigan of the Iron Brigade.* Detroit: Winn & Hammond, 1891.

Dana, Charles A., *Recollections of the Civil War.* New York: D. Appleton and Co., 1898.

Dickert, D. Augustus, *History of Kershaw's Brigade.* Dayton: Morningside Bookshop, 1976.

Donald, David, *Divided We Fought: A Pictorial History of the War 1861-1865.* New York: The Macmillan Co., 1956.

Early, Jubal Anderson, *War Memoirs: Autobiographical Sketch and Narrative of the War between the States.* Ed. by Frank E. Vandiver. Bloomington: Indiana University Press, 1960.

Edwards, William B., *Civil War Guns.* Secaucus, N.J.: Castle Books, 1978.

Elting, John R., and Michael J. McAfee, eds., *Military Uniforms in America.* Vol. 3 of *Long Endure: The Civil War Period, 1852-1867.* Novato, Calif.: Presidio Press, 1982.

Foote, Shelby, *Red River to Appomattox.* Vol. 3 of *The Civil War: A Narrative.* New York: Random House, 1974.

Fox, William F., *Regimental Losses in the American Civil War 1861-1865.* Albany, N.Y.: Albany Publishing Co., 1893.

Frassanito, William A., *Grant and Lee: The Virginia Campaigns 1864-1865.* New York: Charles Scribner's Sons, 1983.

Freeman, Douglas Southall:
Gettysburg to Appomattox. Vol. 3 of *Lee's Lieutenants: A Study in Command.* New York: Charles Scribner's Sons, 1944.
R. E. Lee: A Biography. Vol. 3. New York: Charles Scribner's Sons, 1935.

Fuller, Claud E., and Richard D. Steuart, *Firearms of the Confederacy.* Lawrence, Mass.: Quarterman Publications, 1944.

Gallagher, Gary W., *Stephen Dodson Ramseur: Lee's Gallant General.* Chapel Hill: University of North Carolina Press, 1985.

Gardner, Alexander, *Gardner's Photographic Sketch Book of the Civil War.* New York: Dover Publications, 1959.

Gerrish, Theodore, *Army Life: A Private's Reminiscences of the Civil War.* Portland, Me.: Hoyt, Fogg & Donham, 1882.

Goldsborough, W. W., *The Maryland Line in the Confederate Army: 1861-1865.* Gaithersburg, Md.: Butternut Press, 1983 (reprint of 1900 edition).

Gordon, John B., *Reminiscences of the Civil War.* New York: Charles Scribner's Sons, 1903.

Grant, U. S., *Personal Memoirs of U. S. Grant.* New York: AMS Press, 1972 (reprint of 1894 edition).

Haley, John, *The Rebel Yell & the Yankee Hurrah.* Ed. by Ruth L. Silliker. Camden, Me.: Down East Books, 1985.

Horan, James D., *Timothy O'Sullivan: America's Forgotten Photographer.* New York: Bonanza Books, 1966.

Humphreys, Andrew A., *The Campaign of '64 and '65: The Army of the Potomac, the Army of the James.* Vol. 12 of *Campaigns of the Civil War.* New York: Scribner's Sons, 1883.

Hyde, Thomas W., *Following the Greek Cross: Memories of the Sixth Army Corps.* Boston: Houghton, Mifflin and Co., 1894.

Johnson, Robert Underwood, and Clarence Clough Buel, eds., *Battles and Leaders of the Civil War.* Vol. 4. New York: The Century Co., 1888.

Jordon, Robert Paul, *The Civil War.* Washington, D.C.: The National Geographic Society, 1969.

Ketchum, Richard M., ed., *American Heritage Picture History of the Civil War.* New York: American Heritage Publishing Co., 1960.

Krick, Robert K., *Lee's Colonels: A Biographical Register of the Field Officers of the Army of Northern Virginia.* Dayton: Morningside Bookshop, 1979.

Kunhardt, Dorothy Meserve, Philip B. Kunhardt Jr. and the Editors of Time-Life Books, *Mathew Brady and His World.* Alexandria, Va.: Time-Life Books, 1977.

Lee, Robert E., *The Wartime Papers of R. E. Lee.* Ed. by Clifford Dowdey. New York: Bramhall House, 1961.

Livermore, Thomas L., *Days and Events: 1860-1866.* Boston: Houghton Mifflin Co., 1920.

Lyman, Theodore, *Meade's Headquarters 1863-1865: Letters of Colonel Theodore Lyman from the Wilderness to Appomattox.* Ed. by George R. Agassiz. Boston: Atlantic Monthly Press, 1922.

McAllister, Robert, *The Civil War Letters of General Robert McAllister.* Ed. by James I. Robertson Jr., New Brunswick, N.J.: Rutgers University Press, 1965.

McFeely, William S., *Grant: A Biography.* New York: W. W. Norton & Co., 1981.

McKelvey, Blake, ed., *Rochester in the Civil War.* Rochester, N.Y.: Rochester Historical Society, 1944.

Meredith, Roy, *The World of Mathew Brady: Portraits of the Civil War Period.* Los Angeles: Brooke House Publishers, 1976.

Miller, Delavan S., *Drum Taps in Dixie: Memories of a Drummer Boy 1861-1865.* Watertown, N.Y.: Hungerford-Holbrook Co., 1905.

Miller, Francis Trevelyan, *The Photographic History of the Civil War:*
Vol. 3, *The Decisive Battles.* New York: The Review of Reviews Co., 1911.
Vol. 8, *Soldier Life and the Secret Service.* New York: The Review of Reviews Co., 1912.

Mills, Charles J., *Through Blood and Fire: The Civil War Letters of Major Charles J. Mills 1862-1865.* Comp. and ed. by Gregory A. Coco. Gettysburg: Gregory A. Coco, 1982.

Muffly, J. W., ed., *The Story of Our Regiment: A History of the 148th Pennsylvania Vols.* Des Moines: Kenyon Printing, 1904.

Nichols, G. W., *A Soldier's Story of His Regiment (61st Georgia): And Incidentally of the Lawton-Gordon-Evans Brigade, Army Northern Virginia.* Kennesaw, Ga.: Continental Book Company, 1961.

O'Connor, Richard, *Sheridan: The Inevitable.* Indianapolis: The Bobbs-Merrill Co., 1953.

Patrick, Marsena R., *Inside Lincoln's Army: The Diary of Marsena Rudolph Patrick, Provost Marshal General, Army of the Potomac.* Ed. by David S. Sparks. New York: Thomas Yoseloff, 1964.

Porter, Horace, *Campaigning with Grant*. New York: The Century Co., 1897.

Roe, Alfred Seelye:

The Ninth New York Heavy Artillery. Worcester, Mass.: Privately published, 1899.

The Thirty-Ninth Regiment Massachusetts Volunteers 1862-1865. Worcester, Mass.: Regimental Veteran Assoc., 1914.

Roe, Alfred Seelye, and Charles Nutt, *History of the First Regiment of Heavy Artillery Massachusetts Volunteers: Formerly the Fourteenth Regiment of Infantry 1861-1865*. Mass.: Regimental Association, 1917.

Sanford, George B., *Fighting Rebels and Redskins: Experiences in Army Life of Colonel George B. Sanford 1861-1892*. Ed. by E. R. Hagemann. Norman: University of Oklahoma Press, 1969.

Schaff, Morris, *The Battle of the Wilderness*. Boston: Houghton Mifflin Co., 1910.

Scott, Robert Garth, *Into the Wilderness with the Army of the Potomac*. Bloomington: Indiana University Press, 1985.

Sears, Stephen W., ed., *The American Heritage Century Collection of Civil War Art*. New York: American Heritage Publishing Co., 1974.

Simpson, Harold B., *Hood's Texas Brigade: Lee's Grenadier Guard*. Waco, Tex.: Texian Press, 1970.

Smith, Gene, *Lee and Grant: A Dual Biography*. New York: McGraw-Hill, 1984.

Sorrell, G. Moxley, *Recollections of a Confederate Staff Officer*. Dayton: Morningside Bookshop, 1978.

Starr, Stephen Z., *The War in the East from Gettysburg to Appomattox 1863-1865*. Vol. 2 of *The Union Cavalry in the Civil War*. Baton Rouge: Louisiana State University Press, 1981.

Steere, Edward, *The Wilderness Campaign*. Harrisburg, Pa.: Stackpole Co., 1960.

Stevens, George T., *Three Years in the Sixth Corps*. Albany: S. R. Gray, 1866.

Stiles, Robert, *Four Years under Marse Robert*. Dayton: Morningside Bookshop, 1977 (reprint of 1903 edition).

Tucker, Glenn, *Hancock the Superb*. Dayton: Morningside Bookshop, 1980.

United States War Department, *War of the Rebellion: A Compilation of the Official Records of the Union and Confederate Armies*. Series 1 — Vol. 36, Parts 1 and 3. Washington, D.C.: GPO, 1891-1902.

Vaill, Theodore F., *History of the Second Connecticut Volunteer Heavy Artillery: Originally the Nineteenth Connecticut Vols*. Winsted, Conn.: Winsted Printing Co., 1868.

Wainwright, Charles S., *A Diary of Battle: The Personal Journals of Colonel Charles S. Wainwright 1861-1865*. Ed. by Allan Nevins. New York: Harcourt, Brace & World, 1962.

Waitt, Ernest Linden, comp., *History of the Nineteenth Regiment Massachusetts Volunteer Infantry 1861-1865*. Salem, Mass.: Salem Press, 1906.

Westbrook, Robert S., *History of the 49th Pennsylvania Volunteers*. Altoona, Pa.: Altoona Times, 1898.

Other Sources

Frasca, James C., "The Army Hats of Capt. Charles E. Nash." *North South Trader*, March-April 1978.

"General Grant's Campaign." *Harper's Weekly*, June 4, 1864.

Haines, W. P., "Spotsylvania." *The National Tribune*, January 2, 1890.

Hugunin, George, "At the North Anna." *The National Tribune*, May 26, 1887.

Luvaas, Jay, and Wilbur S. Nye, "The Campaign That History Forgot." *Civil War Times Illustrated*, November 1969.

Matthews, A. E., "Gen. Stuart's Death." *The National Tribune*, June 23, 1887.

Miller, Joseph Michael, "The North Anna River Campaign." Thesis. Virginia Polytechnic Institute, April 1981.

Olcott, Mark, and David Lear, "The Civil War Letters of Lewis Bissell." The Field School Educational Foundation Press, 1981.

Wert, Jeffry, "Spotsylvania: Charge on the Mule Shoe." *Civil War Times Illustrated*, April 1983.

PICTURE CREDITS

INDEX